DON'T PAY ANY FLIGHT SCHOOL MORE THAN $2500 IN ADVANCE

The Censored Information The Bad Guys Don't Want You to Know

Ben Mandell

DON'T PAY ANY FLIGHT SCHOOL MORE THAN $2500 IN ADVANCE
Copyright © 2014 by Ben Mandell

All rights reserved. No part of this book may be reproduced or transmitted in any form or by any means without written permission from the author.

ISBN 978-0615990019

Printed in USA

Dedication

This book is dedicated to the brave aviation folks that came forward with incredibly sensitive information about how pilot flight training has been operating in the United States for the past thirty years.

These brave people put their jobs and their lively hood at risk so that this information could be documented. It is my hope that by furnishing this information to the prospective flight student, whether you are embarking on a hobby or a professional career, that I can stop the bad guys from stealing your dreams.

Knowledge is power.

Table of Contents

Foreword 7
Preface 9
Introduction 11
In The Beginning 13
The Jerks At WEBS.com 21
Why AOPA Sucks 29
Real Stories Of Aussie Air 37
How The Big Scam Works 77
The Fake Scholarship 89
Tips To Save You Money...................... 93
Costs And How To Pay 99
Contracts And Conditions 109
What You Should Consider................ 113
He Who Holds The Gold Rules 125

Foreword

Becoming a pilot can be a wonderful occupation or hobby. Many people have the dream to fly airplanes from the time they are a child. Flying an aircraft is one of the most incredible things that a "regular person" can do in their lifetime.

Flight training is also one of the most expensive educational endeavors that a person can embark on. Flight training can cost more than $70,000 per year in the US. It will also take several years to obtain all of your ratings and hours if you want to become a commercial pilot that transports passengers.

Most people in the aviation training industry are honest hardworking folks. These people have a love for flying and want to pass that knowledge along to future pilots.

Unfortunately there are also some "bad guys" in the aviation training industry. These "bad guys" are bad for the industry and bad for you. If you aren't careful, they will steal your dream and steal your money.

This book will show you how to avoid the bad guys and keep your dream alive.

Preface

Some of the information contained in this book was originally published on the Jet University student website while I was a student at the flight school. It has been reprinted here with permission.

When this information was first gathered together, I had no idea that the students (myself included) had been scammed by a scheme that had been around the flight training industry for over 30 years.

The student website (jetunivesitysucks.com) remained up and active for 5 years until it was censored by WEBS.COM. In late 2013, WEBS.COM took the website down because they deemed the information, that you are about to read, too controversial.

Introduction

Over the next 10 years, the demand for professional airline pilots is going to be greater than anytime in history. There has been talk of a pilot shortage for many years. It has never happened and most people, within the industry, thought it would never happen. Well the pilot shortage has happened and it is here now.

As I write this book in 2014, flights will be canceled this year because there are not enough pilots to fly the commercial airliners. This is creating a demand that the bad guys in the flight training industry will attempt to exploit against those that are unaware of the knowledge which is contained within this book.

My sincere hope is that this book will save you more money on your flight training than any other book that you will come across.

You are to be congratulated for your smart purchase of this book. This book will save you thousands of dollars, in lost tuition, and will help keep your dream alive.

Chapter One

In The Beginning

When I was 10 years old, I had two dreams that would not go away all through my adulthood. It's not unusual for a child to have dreams. It's actually encouraged and considered a healthy sign of growing up.

One of my dreams was to fly jet airplanes. That dream would stay with me my entire life and it has still not gone away. I am pleased to report that that my dream did indeed come true and I hope your dreams come true as well.

This book would never have been published if everything had gone smoothly along the way. After all, there would not have been a reason to write this book!

But as you probably know by now, things in aviation are not always what they seem. This book has the information that you really need, to help you identify when things are just not right. If you pay close attention no one will be able to steal your dream or your money.

If you are reading this you are probably a prospective flight student or are involved in the industry in some form.

If you are one of those flight schools that collects tens of thousands of dollars up front from students, before you furnish the flight training, you are not going to like this book.

The information in this book has been known in the flight training industry for at least three decades. But no one talks about it. No one has ever published how this works. It's one of those dirty secrets that is swept under the rug.

There are those in the industry that believe you will damage your professional pilot career by talking about this "secret" information.

There is a lot of money at stake here. It amounts to millions and millions of dollars each year.

What is sad, is the fact that most people in the flight training industry are honest, hardworking people. They don't realize that the bad guys in the industry are bad for the entire profession. If the industry will eliminate the bad guys from the industry then the honest, hardworking people will benefit as well as the students they teach.

I'm not going to attempt to teach you anything about flying in this book. I'll leave that job to your flight instructor. What I am going to show you is how to save your money and keep your dream from turning into a nightmare.

There are a lot of bad guys that do not want you to know this information.

Over the years, a lot of pilots have lost money on flight training. Some of those pilots think that losing money is equivalent to "paying your dues." The reason they think this way is because that has long been part of the culture of aviation training.

There are a good number of people in this industry that will blame the student for losing his/her money on flight training. They will say you didn't do your homework and check out the flight school. That may or may not be true, but that does not give someone a license to steal your money and your dream.

Most students come into the flight training arena without any knowledge of how this all works. You might be an 18 year old looking at an aviation career. There is no possible way that an 18 year old will have the knowledge to avoid the scams and con men in this industry. It is absolutely impossible.

This book is written for the person that is looking to become a professional commercial pilot. Those that just want to get their private pilot license will also benefit because one day they might want to add to their ratings and become a commercial pilot.

No matter where you go for your flight training, all pilot's licenses look and mean the same. They are all issued by the FAA. No one can tell where, or how much you trained, or how much you spent, simply by looking your pilot's license. No one has a special deal with the FAA to get you a license.

With that being said, there are five ratings that you will be dealing with as you become a commercial pilot. While you may obtain your ratings in various orders and combinations, here is the order that I recommend you obtain these ratings in today's training environment:

1. Private Pilot
2. Instrument Pilot
3. Single Engine Commercial Pilot
4. Multi Engine Add On
5. ATP

Every rating (other than Private Pilot) requires that you have and hold another rating prior to obtaining a subsequent rating. This is a very important point that you need to know.

At the end of your training, In order to fly passengers for an airline you are going to need an ATP (Air Transport Pilot) rating. That currently requires a minimum of 1500 hours of flight time plus some additional training. Getting 1500 hours of flight time is going to take you several years and that is the FAA's intent with this rating.

Everyone must start at the beginning. All pilots must start with the PRIVATE PILOT rating. Once you have your private pilot rating you will be able to fly your friends around with you. However you can't charge them (although they can help pay for gas) and you are not allowed to fly under instrument conditions. You can only fly under VFR (Visual Flight Rules) In effect, you must always be able to see the ground or you can not fly. But this is where everyone starts. **You can not go onto the other ratings until you have your PRIVATE PILOT rating.**

You can obtain your Private Pilot rating at any place that teaches flight training. All Private Pilot licenses are issued by the FAA. It does not matter where you obtain your training as long as you are instructed, and signed off, by an FAA licensed Flight Instructor.

Almost every airport in the US has some sort of flight training available. The exceptions are the larger airports that do not allow student pilots. There are over 5300 paved airports in the US and there is probably one near you that offers some sort of flight training.

I recommend that ALL students obtain their PRIVATE pilot training and license at a <u>local</u> airport. There is no need to move somewhere to get this training. It's expensive and when you move you put yourself under some time pressure and additional added expense that you really do not need.

It's always cheaper to do your training where you are right now. You don't have to move. You don't have to eat out. You don't have to give up your current job. You will also find out if this profession is really for you. Hey if it doesn't work, wouldn't you really want to find out early on before you commit $100,000 (or more) for your flight training?

You can find a local air training facility by calling your local airport and asking them who offers flight training at their airport. It really is that simple. You can also check Craig's List for "flight training" or some similar search term.

Sometimes you may find an independent CFI (flight instructor) that will take students directly and not work through a school. This is a good thing! Sometimes the local crop duster is also a CFI. As long as the CFI has his flight instructor certificate then he is legal to instruct you because he has passed all of the requirements that the FAA mandates that he must have before being issued his flight instructor certificate.

If you are able to find a local CFI and book him directly, it is a win win for both you and the CFI since he does not have to split his pay with a flight school. Flight schools take up to 75% of the pay of their flight instructors. After all they have a business to run!

As you train, keep in mind that every hour your put in your log book counts! If you switch flight instructors or switch schools—you do not lose those hours or any ratings you have already obtained unless you switch to a Part 141 school.

This is an important point that you need to understand. The reason for this is because if you start having issues with your school or your flight instructor, you are able to go to another without penalty unless you have paid in advance or you are switching to a Part 141 school. A Part 141 school will require that you begin a new rating from the beginning. Any other work or flying that you have done towards that rating will not transfer to a Part 141 school, although any hours you have flown may still be logged and count towards your total time.

As you go through this book we are going to tell you to never pay more than $2500 in advance to any flight training facility for any reason no matter what they tell you. This is the most important thing you are going to learn in this book.

No matter what discount they offer, no matter what deal they have, no matter how good they make you feel, NEVER PAY ANYONE MORE THAN $2500 IN ADVANCE FOR ANY FLIGHT TRAINING. No professional airline pilot will ever recommend that you spend more than $2500 in advance.

If you will follow this rule, you will never run into trouble because when the bad guys want to scam you they want a whole lot more than $2500.

You might be surprised to know that most flight schools do not charge anything in advance!

Most flight schools will take you up in the aircraft with an instructor and charge you for the flight when you land and walk back into the office. It's a pay as you go program. You don't fly—you don't pay. If you want to stop then you just stop. There is no penalty. If you run out of money, then you stop until you get some more.

If you find a flight school that wants to collect more than $2500 from you, then you should not consider that school. Again, most schools do not charge anything in advance.

As you read this book, you will find out exactly why these advance payment flight schools are dangerous for you and your career.

In the meantime, before I end this chapter, let me give you an "out of aviation" example of how this might work.

Suppose you like to eat. Pretend a new restaurant was opening up and they had a sample night and you were there. The food looked and tasted pretty good.

But this was a new type of restaurant. This restaurant required that you pay them one year in advance for all of your meals. If you eat 3 meals a day you will need to pay in advance for 1095 meals. The restaurant wants $13,000 in advance for those meals.

You can't get your money back if you don't eat all of the meals. You can't get more than 3 meals per day. You must come only during the posted hours and you will only get one meal every 5 hours.

If you want a larger portion then there is an extra charge. If the restaurant starts serving bad meals to discourage their prepaid customers from showing up—there is nothing you can do about it.

You just lost $13,000. You say you would never do anything like this. You say you are smarter than that. But that is exactly how prepaid aviation schools work.

Chapter Two

The Jerks at WEBS.COM

This chapter is about why this book exists in the first place. It really has nothing to do with flight training and you could skip this chapter if you wish. But you might find this information interesting. You are going to find that I am not going to pull punches. I'm naming names.

In November of 2008, the students at Jet University needed a website to communicate with present and former students because things were not going so well at Jet University for the students. At that time WEBS.com offered a package that worked perfectly for the students. A website was established called jetunivesitysucks.com.

This website quickly became a gathering place for present and former students. We were able to connect students that had been ripped off before us by Jet University.

None of us knew those students existed because Jet University had a business practice of kicking students out of flight school for some trumped up reason and then keeping most of the money that had been paid in advance.

They were able to do this because they had some really unfair written refund policies, buried in their multi-page contract, that allowed the school to keep the most of the student's money if they left school for any reason.

Jet University told the students (that they were ripping off) that they were awful pilots and that they would never make it at the airlines. The end result was these students went home owing $70,000 plus in student loans with no ratings. They felt pretty bad about themselves and they didn't want to discuss it with anyone. Jet University had convinced them that they were failures.

With the jetuniversitysucks.com website we were able to reach out to the former students and start putting the pieces together. At the beginning we did not know this was a scam.

After spending several months gathering the information, we determined that most of us had been scammed. Jet University had collected millions of dollars for prepaid flight training and had not provided the training for over 150 students. Their business model consisted of finding a reason to kick a student out of school and then keeping most of the money.

Jet University also tried to shake us down for additional funds along the way even though we had pre-paid in advance for all of our flight training. When they couldn't get any more money out of us, they would trump up a reason to kick us out.

When the student website went up, we were contacted by students from other flight schools that had experienced similar fates. They had paid in advance and the school had not provided the flight training.

In the end, we determined that this prepaid flight training scam had been going on for at least 30 years in the flight training industry and no one seemed to care or want to do anything about it.

We were able to find some people that did care and we did do something about it. That information is in another chapter.

Back to The Jerks at WEBS.COM

We had no issues with WEBS.com in 2008, 2009, 2010, 2011 and 2012. WEBS.com never contacted us except to send us a bill for fees. (There is also a company called WEB.COM, owned by Network Solutions) and that is not the company we are talking about here)

WEBS.com was started by a couple of brothers in the early 2000's that believed in free speech and free websites. In 2011 Vistaprint.com purchased WEBS.com.

I don't know if the problems we started to have were as a result of the Vistaprint.com purchase, but thinking about their marketing practice of giving away free business cards that really aren't free; it would not surprise me.

In September 2013, we started having trouble with WEBS.com.

WEBS.com froze the Jetuniversitysucks.com website. The website had been up since 2008 and now 5 years later, we are being censored and taken down. We exchanged quite a number of e-mails back and forth over 3 months. I don't have the space to print them all here and you probably wouldn't be interested in them anyway. However there are two that you should know about.

Here is the first e-mail they sent:
**In a message dated 9/9/2013 3:17:04 P.M. Eastern Daylight Time,
abuse@webs.com writes:**

**Dear Webs User,
Webs received written notification that your website contained allegedly defamatory content.
After reviewing your site, Webs determined that the content was in fact defamatory or otherwise objectionable.
Accordingly, pursuant to the Webs Terms of Service, Webs has suspended your website pending the removal of this content.**

http://www.jetuniversitysucks.com/aussieairincstudents.htm

If you believe that the website was suspended mistakenly, and wish to have the content restored, please provide us with the following:

**1. your name, address, phone number, and written or electronic signature;
2. identification of the material that was removed and its location before removal; and
3. a statement explaining under penalty of perjury that the material was removed mistakenly.**

Upon receipt, Webs will review your explanation and, in its sole discretion, will determine whether to restore the website.
Best Regards,
Webs Abuse Department

We went back and forth and their objection to this page was a former home street address of the former owner of Aussie Air Flight School. We removed the street address and the site was restored on October 02, 2013, after being down for three weeks.

On October 23, 2013, the site was taken down again. Keep in mind that we have not changed any of the sections that WEBS.com is complaining about since 2010. All of a sudden 3 years later, we have an issue that is taking the entire site down.

WEBS.com will not take my phone calls and they do not respond immediately to e-mails. It normally takes them at least a week to respond.

On December 19, Clark from WEBS.com responded again:

Clark (Webs Support)

Dec 05 19:01 (EST)

The specific pages the complainants mentioned were the following

www.jetuniversitysucks.com/aussieairincstudents.htm
www.jetuniversitysucks.com/biggestscamintheus.htm
www.jetuniversitysucks.com/aptascam.htm

Please reply.

Those editorial content of those 3 sections are included in the following chapters. The content that is being censored gives us a clue into who has a problem with what we have published.

There are three sections. One of the sections is specifically about the defunct Florida flight school that was known as Aussie Air, Inc.

This flight school came to our attention after they moved into the former Jet University flight school building after Jet University closed. As it turned out, the Aussie Air school was far worse than the Jet University school.

Aussie Air had been in business 7 years and in that time only 2 students had actually finished the school. The rest were ripped off and did not receive all of the flight training they had paid for. Aussie Air was able to operate as long as they did because they would recruit foreign students from Spain that did not know the US laws or know what to do when they had been ripped off.

We were subsequently contacted by the FBI and the Department of Homeland Security regarding Aussie Air. None of the Aussie Air students had the proper flight school Visa and this was a matter of national security.

The second section on Clark's email does not name any specific school or any specific person. The censored sections simply details how the prepaid flight school scam works and how the bad guys are able to pull it off. If anyone is objecting to this section, it could only be because they do not want you to see it! You will see the complete censored sections in the following chapters.

The third section is about a fake pilot scholarship program that the defunct Jet University was attempting to do towards the end of their life. They simply doubled the price of the training and the prospective student would "win" a 50% scholarship to Jet University. Or course the student had to pay the other half **in advance.**

WEBS.com currently will not tell me who is filing these complaints and I don't have the ability to know who the accuser is. I do feel that we will eventually find out who is behind the complaints that WEBS.com should be ignoring or at least try to verify before taking a website down. I have given them the contact information of people that will verify the contents of the website if that is really the problem.

In the meantime if you are thinking about doing business with WEBS.com, you might want to pick another ISP since this company will take your website down just because someone doesn't like what you have to say.

Also if you have been doing business with VISTAPRINT.COM (which now owns WEBS.com), I would appreciate it if you would purchase your "free" business cards and other materials elsewhere until these people come to their senses.

There are a number of companies on the internet that sell the same thing at the same or lower prices. I'm sure some of those people would appreciate your business. Just Google VistaPRINT and you will find their competitors.

28

Chapter 3

Why AOPA sucks

I first joined AOPA (Aircraft Owners and Pilots Association) in 1988 when I received my Private Pilots license. My flight instructor recommended that I join because they were a great organization and they really helped the pilots.

When I went to Jet University to finish up my ratings in 2007, I was a member of AOPA and I purchased life insurance from them while I was in training because my regular life insurance excludes payment if you are killed while doing any flight training.

While I didn't expect to be killed in a training accident, I had a responsibility to my wife and kids that I could not ignore. Fortunately I survived commercial pilot training even though there are some flight school owners that wish that I had not. With that being said, I sure most flight school owners appreciate the efforts that I have made to protect their business and their students from the bad guys in this business.

I also subscribed to the legal plan and the rented aircraft insurance. So I was spending a great deal of money with AOPA insurance services in 2007 and 2008.

I had always considered AOPA as my friend. They would take care of my pilot issues if there was a problem although I had never called them for any help.

So it was natural that in the summer of 2008 when students were not receiving the training at Jet University, that we had paid for, that the first organization that I would call would be "my friends" at AOPA. They would know what to do and they would surely provide the needed guidance and help that we needed. After all we were card carrying AOPA members!

It turns out that I wasn't the first student to contact AOPA about flight schools ripping of students by not providing the flight training and keeping the students money.

AOPA had been receiving these calls for many years. Yet AOPA had not done anything about these calls. The nice people at AOPA told me that they had heard this story over and over and they were very sorry to hear of my troubles. But, because the laws did not require the flight schools to protect the students tuition, there really wasn't anything they could do to help us.

AOPA suggested I need to work on changing the laws to prevent this from happening in the future. Of course this was simply lip service and they never expected that I would actually try to change the laws.

What the people at AOPA did not know is that it had been many years, but I did have experience in getting laws changed.

To understand how to change laws, you first must determine who would enforce and oversee any proposed laws.

My first contact was the FAA. What I learned was the FAA has absolutely no interest in regulating flight schools. They have never done it and they are not about to start looking at financial statements, insurance policies and surety bonds. The FAA has enough work to do and they are not interested in getting any more work.

Most flight schools operate under part 61 and the FAA does not regulate them or even know who they are. The FAA does not have a list of these flight schools. Most part 61 flight schools are honest. However the flight schools that have been taking students money and not providing the flight training are able to do this under part 61 without any regulation or registration requirements from the FAA.

Less than 10% of the flight schools in the US are Part 141 schools. The FAA does know who the part 141 flight schools are because they do look over their courses and training. However the FAA does not look at their financial records to even determine if these schools are stable. The FAA will not handle any consumer issues (such as lost tuition) A school can lose their 141 status and remain open as a part 61 school and you would not be able to tell the difference.

Again keep in mind that your pilot's license will look the same no matter what type of school you obtained your training at. (part 61 or part 141)

That leaves the regulation solely to the States. The most popular states for flight training are Arizona, California, Florida and Texas.

The reason for this is because the weather is more favorable, in those states, for flight training on a year round basis. In other words there are more available flight days in those states than in other states. For this reason there are also more airports in those states and more flight training facilities in those states.

Flight training is considered for profit vocational training in most instances. Unless the flight training program is part of a college or university, you will not receive a college degree when you finish your flight training. The company that teaches you expects to make a profit off of you. You are their customer.

There are many vocational training programs in every state in the United States. Other vocational training programs that you might be aware of are from a truck driving school, cosmetology school, IT school or bar tending school. Flight training happens to be the most expensive vocational training.

Vocational schools are usually regulated by some sort of post secondary educational commission in each state.

The educational commissions are used to regulating for profit vocational schools. The commissions generally have the financial requirements, bonding requirements, regulations and insurance requirements already in place.

In every state that we were interested in, the flight schools were exempt (by state laws) from any regulation by the state post secondary commissions.

Some unknown organization had been very successful, many years ago, in getting flight schools exempt from any state regulation in almost every state. That took someone a lot of work and a lot of money.

That exemption was allowing the bad guys to operate prepaid flight school tuition scams with absolutely no oversight and no regulation. After a student had been scammed, there was nothing he could do about it.

I was curious about who might have been able put these exemptions in place. I thought it might be AOPA. They indicated that it was not them and they really did not know who did it. They claimed they did not know why these exemptions were even in place.

It was obvious that what needed to be done was to get that state exemption deleted in each of the states and let the state post secondary education commissions regulate flight schools so that the student tuition would be protected.

Surely AOPA would be helpful in getting this exemption deleted and getting the student tuition protected. After all they were friends of the pilots. They wouldn't want to see student pilots continue to lose millions of dollars each year, would they?

So I targeted the four most popular states (Arizona, California, Florida and Texas), for flight training, and attempted to get the laws changed so that the student tuition is protected. I really didn't care about anything other than to make sure the tuition is protected. I figured if the tuition is protected then the rest would take care of itself.

The first state I worked on was Florida. To this day, Florida still does not protect student tuition. I do believe they will get to it one day. When I contacted them, the head of the post secondary educational commission was getting ready to retire (in less than a year) and he had absolutely no interest in helping push this initiative forward.

I contacted the other states. We started to get some traction in California and I am happy to report that we were successful in California in getting student tuition protected. Governor Arnold Schwarzenegger signed the law into effect. It took a lot of work. It took a lot of attending committee hearings. I called on my fellow Jet University students to come to the hearings and testify about their tuition losses.

The most disappointing thing, to me, during all of this political work was that the Jet University students were the only ones speaking up to protect the students tuition. No one cared about the students. Dozens of people would blame the students for losing their money instead of the bad guys that actually stole it from them.

I would go into a hearing with dozens of people and everyone, except the Jet University students, would try to convince the politicians and regulators that there was no problem.

The saddest day in all of this for me was when AOPA sent their representatives to these hearings to lobby for not changing the laws and not protecting the student tuition. They did this in California and in Arizona. My "friends" at AOPA let me down and they let every student pilot in this country down. For this reason, I no longer belong to AOPA and every time I get a chance, I recommend that others not renew their membership in AOPA.

There is an organization called NATA. That is the National Air Transport Association. I later found out that NATA was the organization responsible for getting the state exemptions into law that prohibited states from regulating flight schools. This allowed the bad guys to steal millions of dollars in student tuition over the past 30 plus years.

NATA incorrectly represented, that the flight schools were being regulated by the FAA when they were not being regulated by anyone at all.

In one of the hearings in California, one of the assemblymen indicated that they all thought the flight schools were being regulated by the FAA (as NATA had incorrectly represented) and it was never their intention that flight schools not be regulated. California now regulates flight schools and protects student tuition as does Utah and Tennessee.

We went to Arizona and we were able to convince the post secondary educational commission to call a hearing to examine why flight schools in Arizona were not being regulated even though there has been a law on the books since 1975 requiring them to do so.

AOPA and NATA were there fighting us as usual. AOPA and NATA were able to convince the regulators in Arizona that flight schools in Arizona were NOT vocational schools for the professional pilot. They were merely "hobby schools" and not vocational schools.

Flight school students had lost 35 million dollars at Arizona "hobby schools" during the prior 5 years and the commission did nothing about it. Thanks AOPA.

If you want to be a professional pilot, then you should not go to Arizona for training until they start enforcing the laws, that are already in place, to protect the professional pilot student tuition.

In the end this is all about money. The bad guys join NATA and AOPA and they are a revenue source for NATA and AOPA. The bad guys buy ads in their magazines. The bad guys spend money on fuel with NATA members. They buy or lease aircraft from NATA members. Everyone wants the scam to continue because they make a lot of money off of the bad guys.

On the other hand, students are not spending money with NATA members. They aren't buying ads in the AOPA or NATA magazine. So the students get no representation. So the scam continues until the students have the knowledge and power to stop the insanity and stop paying tuition money in advance to flight schools.

One day I hope AOPA will be my friend again. That will be the day, we all are on the same side of the table protecting student tuition. That will be the day we both can go to the other popular flight training states (Arizona, Florida and Texas) and help get the laws changed to protect flight school student tuition. That is the right thing to do and that is what I thought my friend was doing all along.

Chapter Four

Real Stories of Aussie Air

What you are about to read is true. The names have not been changed. All of this really did happen to flight school students attending a flight school.

This very same scam has happened at MANY flight schools in the United States over the past 30 years. I could list dozens of schools that have collected large pre-paid flight school tuition and not provided the training to the students.

However, for this book, I'm just going to detail one school. If I detailed any of the other schools, the story would end the very same way.

Aussie Air was made up of mostly foreign students. However the scam works the same with schools made up of American students. The students at Aussie Air went though the same thing that thousands of us had already gone through at American schools.

Many American flight schools will switch over to recruiting foreign students when they no longer attract American students. Jet University did that towards the end of their life. The American schools are interested in foreign students because they collect the flight school tuition in advance from the foreign students.

After Jet University shut down in May of 2009, another flight school decided to move from Daytona Beach, FL to Ft Lauderdale.

The flight school was Aussie Air. We had never heard of Aussie Air although they had been in business since 2004. They came to our attention when they moved into the former Jet University building.

Aussie Air did not recruit American students. They only recruited foreign students. Most of the students were from Spain.

The way Aussie Air worked was that they advertised and recruited in Spain. They would collect half of the money upfront in Spain and the second half when the student arrived in the United States.

Aussie Air used an illegal VISA scheme to indicate that the students were coming to America to learn English rather than to participate in flight training.

After the 911 attacks, the Department of Homeland Security required that all VISAS for flight training must come through them. No Aussie Air student ever received a proper flight training VISA. We were later contacted by the FBI and Department of Homeland Security about this.

When Aussie Air moved into the building we did not know what was going on. We didn't know if the former officials at Jet University had a connection with Aussie Air.

We set out to find out all we could about Aussie Air. At the time the school moved to Ft Lauderdale, it was 6 years old. The word around the Daytona airport was that they were several months behind on their rent there. That was already a bad sign.

They were in a much smaller facility in Daytona of less than 1500 square feet which they could not afford to pay the rent on. They were moving into a 20,000 square foot facility in Ft Lauderdale with a monthly rent that would cost more than 10 times what they were supposed to be paying in Daytona.

We were having a very hard time getting information about Aussie Air. Aussie air management knew that we were looking around. They told the students not to talk to us. They even made threats against the students if they did speak with any of us.

They made death threats against me. On one call, I told the owner of the school if he could show me that he was protecting the students tuition that I would support him. He obviously could not do that.

Aussie Air made a serious mistake that would open the doors up to all of the information we needed to know about them. When they Aussie Air left Daytona, they failed to pay the employees that had worked for them in Daytona.

Those employees would later come forward and direct us to the information we were looking for.

Only two students had ever finished all of their ratings at Aussie Air. One of the students that finished was one of the girlfriends of the son of the owner. I don't know who the other was and It's not important. But with a six year track record with only two students actually completing the training, this school was much worse than Jet University.

Aussie Air students started to contact us. We were able to keep their identities private. The management at Aussie Air kept threatening the students. They would kick them out of school if they talked to us. They put out a reward of extra flight hours if anyone would let them know who was talking with us. It was a very difficult time for the students.

Although Aussie Air was one of the worst examples of flight schools stealing money from students; they were not the only one and they would not be the last. I'm sure the guys that ran Aussie Air will try to get back into the flight school business at some point. After all it's easy money to them.

We kept a running blog section on the jetuniversitysucks.com website just for the Aussie Air students. This section will give you an idea of what the Aussie Air flight school students were going through.

As you read the blog, try to put yourself it the student's place and in his mind. Imagine if this were happening to you after you had prepaid tens of thousands of dollars in advance for flight training.

This is real and this actually did happen. It is published in the order that it happened, from the newest to the oldest.

This is the section that WEBS.COM censored and does not want you do see:

Aussie Air Finally Hits The Papers

We first reported Aussie Air closed on March 1, 2010.

On September 9, 2010, the Florida Sun Sentinel wrote a story about Aussie Air. They used our website as a resource and pretty much repeated what we had published 6 months earlier.

AUSSIE AIR CLOSED

03/01/10. Aussie Air announced, to the students today, that they are shutting down effective immediately. Our best estimate is that students have lost at least FOUR MILLION DOLLARS at Aussie Air.

Aussie Air was started in 2004 and has had at least 3 different locations. Each "move" left students without their training and employees without their paychecks.

In the summer of 2009, Aussie Air moved into the former Jet University building and that is when they came under our radar. It was obvious from the very beginning that this simply was not going to work.

Sheltaire is the landlord at KFXE and Sheltaire must take some responsibility for putting Aussie Air in a 20,000 square foot building that they could not possibly afford. A simple check with the prior landlord in Daytona Beach would have turned up that Aussie Air was five months past due on their rent for a much smaller space. This was common knowledge around the airport and even the Sheltaire employees at KDAB knew this.

And then we have to question why a company like Premier Aviation would leaseback planes to Aussie Air when they had full knowledge that two companies had already repossessed their other planes because they were not paid for. Word on the street is that Premier has now lost $30,000 when they took back the Aussie Air leaseback planes because they were past due.

Is this business so devoid of scruples that companies like Sheltaire and Premier Aviation simply look the other way? We absolutely know both of these companies had full knowledge of what was going on here.

In the almost seven (7) years Aussie Air was in business, we have found only two students actually graduated and received all of the training they had paid for.

Aussie Air was a scam and it is amazing they were able to continue this scam for almost seven (7) years.

It is past time for regulating flight schools in the State of Florida.

Luis Vargas Martinez using other names to continue the scam

Luis Vargas Martinez is also using the name Luis Sotomayor to market flight school programs. Don't be fooled!

Beware of Luis Sotomayor!

Mr. Luis Osvalco Vargas Martinez rented a home at Parkland Golf & Country Club

It appears that Mr Luis Osvalco Vargas Martinez lived quite well at the golf course home located at CENSORED Satin Leaf Place, Parkland, FL 33076.

The home rents for $3950 a month and we understand that Mr. Vargas handed the rental agent from Solid Rock Realty, Inc, $12,000 cash in order to move in.

The home, built in 2006, is located in the most upscale and prestigious area of Broward according to the real estate agent. It features a swimming pool, marble floors, gourmet kitchen, granite counters, stainless steel appliances as well as a deluxe master suite.

Are They Moving Or Are They Shutting Down?

We have learned Aussie Air has been given notice by the landlord (Sheltaire) to vacate the building by this Wednesday due to unpaid rent. Students are moving out of the building. This is the same thing that happened last year in Daytona. We're starting to see a pattern here. Don't landlords check tenants out anymore before they allow them to move into a building?

So the question remains, are they moving or are they shutting down? If they are moving then why do they need to sell all of this stuff? Why would they sell their Ford Focus and golf carts? Seems like you might need those things if you are planning to stay in business.

Who would rent to these guys when they have a history of leaving landlords without paying the rent?

Who would lease planes to this outfit when they have a history of having them repossessed from multiple lenders?

Things are stinking up at Aussie Air and FXE Flight Center

02/20/10 We are getting reports that the water bill has not been paid and there has been no water for showers, flushing toilets, brushing teeth, etc for the past four days at the Aussie Air FXE Flight Center building. This includes the dorms. It looks like they are selling merchandise out in front of the building. Also notice the name of the flight school has been removed from the canopy.

Most of the planes have been repossessed again. There are only two airplanes left. One remaining plane is 787HC which is owned by Heath Cohen the owner of Jet University.

It's obvious these guys are just about done.

The moral of the story is don't pay any flight school more than $2500 in advance and don't ever let them get more than $2500 ahead of you in undelivered courses or services no matter how good they make it sound and no matter what guarantee they give you.

And Luis O Vargas Martinez starts yet another flight school

First it was Aussie Air. Then it was ILI Flight School. Then it was FXE Flight Center. And now the flight school of the month is FLY NOW EXPRESS INC.

It's getting hard to keep up with all of the names this outfit has.

Another Aussie Air Student that lost his money

This is another letter we received at jetuniversitysucks.com this past week from an Aussie Air student:

I saw this school beginning of summer 2009.

After contacting the school, Mr. Luis O Vargas Martinez, offered me 156 hours for $10,000. He obviously did the best offer in USA like always. (editor's note: That is $64.10 per air hour with instructor for plane and fuel)

For me it was not possible a price like that, but to make sure I fell on this scam, Mr. Luis Vargas called me very often, telling me how good his school was, and making false promises.

After numerous calls, and emails, in which he painted his school as the best place, I decided why not? He seemed to be so honest, that I never thought about looking up in the internet who he really was.

I paid him through a wire-transfer US $10,000 on august 2009, the same month I got there. I was there for a month, only flew 1.3 Hours.

He did a written contract, in which he compromised to refund my money back (US$9300) in 30 days to my account. He NEVER DID, excuses and lies, every time I called.

After I got there I started to see that everything was a lie. Stories from each and every single student that talked to me where the same. SCAM SCAM!! There was a few student that were scare of the Vargarism, because they usually intimidate the students a lot, and those were the only one who was silent. Anything that goes against the "SPIRIT of AUSSIE AIR" and you are OUT of the school.

They told me they had 9 aircraft, in the time I was there, they only had 4 old Cessna. Mr Luis Vargas Martinez told me I would fly at least 3 to 4 times a week by phone, the contract said 7 months; I repeat only 1.3 in one month.

These people are scammers, lairs, they don't care nothing about their students. They just want to steal the money away from students. That's all. They even intimidate students who talk to Jetuniversitysucks.com, bla bla...

Don't believe anything MR LUIS O VARGAS MARTINEZ promises or writes in his contract, they are all a LIE. When you ask for your money back, so you can go fast, he will do you a contract promising to refund your money in 30 days, its a LIE, is only so you can go fast and the others never know.

They don't pay instructor, my instructor there left, because he was not paid for his work. Other instructor had to call the police so they can get paid. They give checks with no funds!. After the instructor goes, they say that they fired him, because he or she was stealing money from the school!! They told me that about my instructor, who was a good instructor.

MR Luis O Vargas told me personally once, in the attitude of intimidating me, that when student piss him off, he just simply doesn't put them to fly, so that they spend all their money and go back home

I really hope no one falls on his contract, and that what happened to me saves other people money from falling on Luis O Vargas Martinez hands or any of his Vargarism family. I will also like to see the day when in someway, Mr. Vargas pays for what he has done to all the students he has stolen money.

It is so sad to see how these people can drive BMW, and have a good life, with the money they steal or scam from student.

MR Luis O Vargas Martinez is definitely a BAD person, and a Liar!.

I will soon be giving documentation to upload to Face book to prove this is true!

Sincerely
Aussie Air student

Aussie Air Attorney furnished a list of over 70 students that did not receive their training.

02/20/10 On November 05, 2009 we furnished a very detailed list of over 70 students to Gabriel Jose Carrera, Esq (Mr. Luis Vargas's attorney) that had not received what they had paid for at Aussie Air. It's been almost four months and we haven't heard from Mr. Carrera.

WAIT THERE'S MORE FROM AUSSIE AIR AND FXE FLIGHT CENTER!

Our investigators have discovered that Mr. Luis Vargas Martinez has started yet another flight school in addition to Aussie Air and FXE Flight Center. All of the "flight schools" are located at the same building and at the same address.

No folks, we aren't making this stuff up. It's getting more and more bizarre. I fully expect Mr. Vargas to start offering Helicopter flight training next since that seems to be the next big flight school scam. The name of the latest flight school is: Isi Airline Academy, Inc.

Mr Luis Vargas Martinez appears to be "opening" a new flight school about once a month in an effort to take the heat off of his business practices. Don't be fooled by ISI Airline Academy! It's the same old Luis Vargas Martinez stuff with a new web page. Beware of ISI AIRLINE ACADEMY! Don't join the FLIGHT SCHOOL OF THE MONTH program. Read the whole Aussie Air page below.

DO NOT GIVE THESE PEOPLE (or any other flight school) MORE THAN $2500 IN ADVANCE UNDER ANY CIRCUMSTANCES.

NO MATTER HOW MUCH OF A DISCOUNT THEY OFFER,

NO MATTER WHAT NAME THEY CALL THEMSELVES,

NO MATTER HOW GOOD THEY MAKE IT SOUND. DON'T PAY ANY FLIGHT SCHOOL MORE THAN $2500 IN ADVANCE!

DO NOT LET ANY FLIGHT SCHOOL GET MORE THAN $2500 AHEAD OF YOU, FOR UNDELIVERED SERVICES EVER!

AUSSIE AIR CONTINUES WITH A NEW NAME

Our opinion is the heat is getting a little hot for Mr. Luis Vargas Martinez with Aussie Air. So in order to start all over again and collect more money from students, he has started a new flight school at the same location!

They are offering a 100% REFUND AND MONEY BACK GUARANTEE. Don't fall for this unless they are willing to deposit the money in a trust account with a Florida attorney.

There is another school in Florida (Epic Aviation) that has the same 100% guarantee and when the students ask for a refund they don't have the money.

The name of the new school is FXE FLIGHT CENTER INC and the website is www.fxefc.com.

DO NOT GIVE THESE PEOPLE (or any other flight school) MORE THAN $2500 IN ADVANCE UNDER ANY CIRCUMSTANCES.

NO MATTER HOW MUCH OF A DISCOUNT THEY OFFER,

NO MATTER WHAT NAME THEY CALL THEMSELVES,

NO MATTER HOW GOOD THEY MAKE IT SOUND. DON'T PAY ANY FLIGHT SCHOOL MORE THAN $2500 IN ADVANCE!

DO NOT LET ANY FLIGHT SCHOOL GET MORE THAN $2500 AHEAD OF YOU, FOR UNDELIVERED SERVICES EVER!

Actual Student Nightmares from Aussie Air

10/15/2009 We are getting a lot of hits and e-mails regarding Aussie Air over the past few days. We are starting to see a pattern here. Please read this whole page so you can see the pattern for yourself

The nightmare begins when Mr. Vargas quotes an unbelievable price for a flight training program or a time building program that he has proven by his past actions that he will not be able to honor.

After a student is hooked and signs up for the classes, the money is collected upfront in Spain. The student leaves Spain and arrives in Florida to begin classes or time building. Aussie Air then starts to string the students along, slowing them down, not allowing flights and blames the student for some sort of "trumped up" problem to justify this scheme. The end result is that many students lose their money, do not get their ratings and/or do not get their flight time Here are a couple of e-mails (identifying information has been removed to protect the students) from actual Aussie Air students:

Hello, I would like you to know that me and another friend of mine paid to Mr Luis O, Vargas Martinez the amount of 10.000 euros for the following:

FAA PLUS JAA COMMERCIAL WITH 500 HOURS IN 12 MONTHS. ONLY 10 THOUSAND EUROS!!!!!!!!!!

I arrived in early 2009 with my friend and I have to leave the school after spend 8 months and complete only 39.9 hours. and not even get the private pilot license.

THAT IS WHAT MR VARGAS DOES : HE SELLS A TRAINING THAT IS IMPOSSIBLE TO PROVIDE AT THIS PRICE. JUST BECAUSE HE NEEDED THE CASH.

Simply put, he steals the money (we paid in advance) and then he lets us lose our time without doing anything nothing during months.

PLEASE FEEL FREE to contact me for more details,

Thanks a lot

Dear Students,

In the past month of July/August I had with Aussie Air the same troubles that you had and are having.

I lose more than 6,000 USD renting an aircraft for building hours. Vargas Martines didn't even have the aircraft I rented and after 3 weeks I had to rent an aircraft from another school.

Aussie Air didn't return back to me the money I paid.

---

hello i like you to say that AUSSIE AIR GAVE ME DISCOUNT OF 50 PERCENT, 300 HOURS FLYING IN 5000 US DOLLAR, IS IT GOOD?

Hi,how are you? I am an Aussie Air student. I already paid for everything,which is 30,000 euros. I paid half before coming here and the rest 5 days after i arrived in at the school.

That's how it was written in my contract, I then realized how bad things were and that my contract would never be fine for both parts,only for Aussie.

I contracted for 530 hours to receive PPL,IR,CPL and multi and the conversion in Spain in 7-8 months, This is all written in my contract. I'm already here for almost 3 months and i just have 4.6 hours. Now we don't have instructors anymore,just the chief pilot so we can't take any class.

There are many students who would like to get their money back and get into another school or just go back to Spain. I know for sure they are not gonna give me back my money although it's written also in the contract.

People here is really afraid because you can get be out of the school just to talk bad in internet boards. They check your IP or begin to ask the students who it was or the owner ask somebody that if he tells him what it was,he'll give you for free 200 hours. That's the way they are, It's like kind of mafia.

Anyhow,there are lot of things i can explain you. We are here worst than in a jail,no kitchen,no microwave,it's forbidden to have food anywhere here,only of you pay the amount of $100 per month to have a fridge. But i don't mind that if i would be flying, taking classes and everything. I'm just spending money here and not making progress.

These e-mails are representative of the e-mails we have received at jetuniversitysucks.com. Based upon these types of e-mails, and the lack of demonstrated financial stability, we can not recommend any student enroll or do business with Aussie Air until these issues are resolved and the students money is protected against loss.

There are many flight schools in Florida. Please do not pay more than $2500 in advance to any flight school. You see what happens when the school has your money. You are trapped. The school doesn't have the resources to refund. It's almost like being in jail.

Mr. Vargas continues to intimidate Aussie Air Students

10/11/2009 Mr. Vargas and his relatives continue to try to intimidate students and those that speak the truth regarding Aussie Air.

In interviews with students and employees we have determined these threats have been "business as usual" at Aussie Air for many years Mr. Vargas has threatened students and employees by mentioning his lawyer many times

Up until now he has been able to scare the students and employees into remaining silent. Now that students and employees realize what has really been going on they are bravely speaking out about what has happened at Aussie Air.

The simple fact is that lawyers cost a lot of money and they don't work for free How can Mr. Vargas afford to pay a high priced lawyer when he doesn't pay his employees, his insurance bill or his phone bill? A lawyer in Florida is going to cost Mr. Vargas far more than the amount he owes all of his employees put together. Lawyers don't work for free.

He now claims that the Federal Court in Miami is coming after students, employees and this website. This is simply not true and is another of Mr. Vargas's deceptions.

In spite of all of Mr. Vargas's threats about having a lawyer all of these years--no student has ever been contacted by a lawyer. We have yet to hear from any of Mr. Vargas's lawyers here at Jetuniversitysucks.com. We have been hoping to hear from some Aussie Air lawyer so that we can get some help to get the employees paid and the students refunded their money for training that was not provided.

Mr. Vargas does threaten to "take away" paid for flight hours from the students if they speak out, post on a website, contact the better business bureau, contact the police or even talk to this website. Of course since Mr. Vargas has has a history of not providing the hours purchased by students anyway, it is just a matter of time before he decides that you have lost your hours for one trumped up reason or another.

In the past, posts and comments about Aussie Air have been removed from online aviation posting boards in Spain. We are told the reason for this is because Mr. Vargas and his associates control some of the Spanish boards that attract flight students. We think there is a better explanation.

Our opinion is that Mr. Vargas knows his way around posting boards and knows exactly how the rules work and is able to use those rules to have unflattering posts removed. Sometimes a, "report this post" button is all it takes to have a post removed. If you are posting on these other boards, please make sure you are following the rules If you do this then your post has a better chance of staying up.

Mr. Vargas may also have used some intimidation methods against webmasters of aviation boards that he does not control to intimidate those webmasters into removing non flattering posts about Aussie Air. Students allege Aussie Air has caused false recommendations, to be posted, regarding Aussie Air on aviation boards.

We remain firm in our recommendation to NOT PAY AUSSIE AIR ANY MONEY IN ADVANCE no matter how good they make it sound and no matter what discounts they offer you for paying in advance or for paying quickly.

If you are an Aussie Air student that has not received what you paid for or an employee that has not been paid as agreed, please feel free to contact us at: jetustudent@gmail.com

All inquires are held in strict confidence and not shared with the management, students or employees of Aussie Air.

The lies and deception continue at Aussie Air

09/30/2009 Yesterday during the student meeting, Mr. Vargas claimed that he is in communication with this website and that this website is letting him know who is communicating with us.

THIS IS SIMPLY NOT TRUE. We have a policy of not letting any other student or employee know who communicates with us at jetuniversitysucks.com. This has been our policy since this site was started in November, 2008.

Yes there are lots of Aussie Air students and employees that have communicated with us and continue to communicate with us here at jetuniversitysucks.com. That's how we found out about the meeting yesterday!

No, we will not tell you or anyone else (including Mr. Vargas) who communicates with us.

Feel free to contact us at jetustudent@gmail.com.

All inquiries and information is always held in strict confidence.

Aussie Air Specials--Warning Desperation

Aussie Air is offering a desperation special of an FAA license (doesn't say what kind) with 256 hours (doesn't say what kind of hours) for $25,000 if you sign up by October 1, 2009.

Don't do it! Don't pay these guys any money in advance. This is not only laughable, but it is sad because someone is probably going to buy into it. Don't be fooled. Remember they promised they would be a"pay as you go" flight school??????

You can get your FAA private license at just about any FBO and many flight schools for less than $10,000 and you can pay as you go. You can add an instrument rating to the private for another $10,000 (or less) at most FBO's or flight schools.

AUSSIE AIR PHONE HAS BEEN RE-CONNECTED!

Looks like Aussie Air paid the phone bill and had the phone re-connected! Nice work!

Let's celebrate the re-connection of the phone of Aussie Air!

AUSSIE AIR PHONE 954-492-2828 DISCONNECTED

09/22/09. The main phone number at Aussie Air 954-492-2828 has been temporarily disconnected.

AUSSIE AIR LOOKING FOR CFI CFII FLIGHT INSTRUCTORS

Since all of the flight instructors have left Aussie Air because they have not been paid, Aussie Air is now running some ads advertising for more flight instructors.

If you want to work for free and not get paid like the KFXE and KDAB Aussie Air Flight Instructors then please apply right away to Aussie Air at KFXE.

AUSSIE AIR DESPERATE FOR MONEY--WILL BEAT ANYONE'S PRICE

Aussie Air advertises that they will beat anyone's price.

And they will!

No matter what price you find they will beat it!

Our opinion is that it's pretty easy to beat anyone's price when you have a history of not providing the flight training that the students have purchased.

Please do not give Aussie Air any more money.

According to former and present Aussie Air students, any money you turn over to Aussie Air is gone forever. You will not get it back. Do not be fooled.

AUSSIE AIR STUDENTS ARE BEING TOLD TO LEAVE

We are hearing that Aussie Air students in Ft Lauderdale are being told to leave the school for various "trumped up" reasons. Aussie Air appears to be desperate for money and when they can't shake the students down for any more "extra charges", they kick the students out of school.

If you are an Aussie Air student that has been kicked out of the school and you want to finish your ratings, please contact us immediately at jetustudent@gmail.com. Please include your phone number. We will attempt to find you some assistance to help you finish up your ratings.

Our advice remains to not pay any more money to Aussie Air no matter what they promise you. Their history is not looking promising for the students.

ALL AUSSIE AIR FLIGHT INSTRUCTORS HAVE LEFT THE BUILDING

09/10/09 All of the Ft Lauderdale Aussie Air Flight Instructors have walked off of the job because they have not been paid. These Aussie Air Flight Instructors join the ranks of the Aussie Air Daytona Beach Flight Instructors that have not been paid in over 3 months.

It is obvious to those of us on the outside that Aussie Air does not have the money to pay their employees or their current bills and we question their viability as a continuing business.

Students are now in the dorms without classes and without flights. In speaking with several students we have put together an outline of how Aussie Air has operated.

The Aussie Air students are recruited in Spain by Mr. Vargas's father. A program example would be that a student pays 33,000 euros (about $50,000) and is promised 530 flight hours and ratings of Private Pilot, Instrument Pilot, Commercial Pilot and Multi Engine rating.) They are then supposed to get their license converted in Spain upon completion of this program in 7-9 months. We can't find anyone that has completed the program in 7-9 months or in the 18 months that Aussie Air also refers to.

Half of the money is paid in Europe prior to arrival in the US. This is a big mistake and you should never pay this kind of money in advance for flight training to any flight school.

Students arrive in the US and the other half of the money is due within 5 days. Aussie Air does offer a written refund policy, but they do not honor that policy and we have spoken with many students that have requested a refund but have not received it

Once students are here in the US, Aussie Air tries to slow them down. Aussie Air management will determine the students do not speak English properly and not allow the students to fly. As Aussie Air slows the students down, they start to charge additional fees for dorm and food because they say it is now taking longer than expected. It's also a whole lot less expensive to keep these students grounded rather than flying airplanes. This has the effect of frustrating students and making them feel like they are not making progress because of their perceived deficiencies.

We have not yet met any Aussie Air student that has actually finished the Aussie Air course and received their ratings and their licenses in the 7-9 month time that Aussie Air represents. We have heard from many students that have not received their flight time and their licenses. We have also heard of one female student that has finished after 2 1/2 years and over $150,000 in Aussie Air fees.

We are also being told that Aussie Air management has ordered students not to post on blogs, boards, the internet, etc or they will be kicked out of school. They have been told not to talk to us here at jetuniversitysucks.com. Mr. Vargas has also offered a reward of 200 flight hours for anyone that will tell him who has been talking to us. Of course no one would ever get the 200 flight hours because there isn't any gas in the planes!

We stand by our recommendation to not pay Aussie Air any money in advance.

This history of Aussie Air indicates that it is not adequately funded.

This five year history of this flight school shows that most students entering Aussie Air are not able to complete their ratings.

AUSSIE AIR FLEET GROUNDED AGAIN

09/09/09 The Aussie air fleet had flown a limited number of times over the past two weeks since the planes were moved from DAB to FXE. However flying has now come to an end because the fuel bill has not been paid and Banyan will not fuel the planes until the bill is paid.

THE AIRCRAFT AUSSIE AIR DIDN'T MOVE

The aircraft is tail number N7420J which is a 1968 PIPER ARROW. It was not moved this past weekend from DAB to

FXE because it had been prop locked by the leaseback owner after he found out that Aussie Air did not have the proper insurance on the aircraft.

Planes moved today from DAB to FXE!

08/22/09. The Aussie Air planes were moved this morning from DAB to FXE. There is a PIPER ARROW that was not moved because it has a PROP LOCK on it.

The planes had been parked at Precision Air in Daytona since July 10, 2009. We do not know if Aussie Air has obtained insurance on the aircraft at this time. If you are a student at Aussie Air, please make sure the aircraft(s) have the proper insurance in place before you fly them. Also if you let us know when the planes do get the proper insurance we will post it.

Aussie Air Students have not flown since July 10, 2009

August 16, 2009. We are hearing from several current Aussie Air students confirming that no Aussie Air student has flown since July 10, 2009. That is over 36 days of not being able to fly. This is obviously not good for your training.

We are strongly recommending that any Aussie Air student NOT DEPOSIT ANY MORE MONEY with Aussie Air until this school is more stabilized.

If you are a current Aussie Air student and you are stuck in Daytona or in Ft Lauderdale please let us know by sending an e-mail to: jetustudent@gmail.com

BEWARE OF AUSSIE AIR, INC

Beware of paying Aussie Air, Inc (or any flight school) more than $2500 in advance for anything. Insist on a "PAY AS YOU GO" enrollment. Do not let Aussie Air, Inc. (or any flight school) ever get ahead of you by more than $2500. Also check to make sure the flight school has the proper insurance coverages on the aircraft and the facilities. Do not sign up or attend a flight school that does not have the proper insurance coverages.

Aussie Air, Inc has been closed in Daytona Beach for several weeks. Rent has not been paid. Instructors and students have not been able to fly. These students and instructors had no notice of this shut down and are not quite sure what to do while they are grounded.

Aussie Air is presently moving to Fort Lauderdale. Please thoroughly check this school out, WITH FORMER STUDENTS, THE BETTER BUSINESS BUREAU, AND THE LINKS BELOW prior to making a decision about attending.

We do understand that Aussie Air, Inc is now accepting students on a "PAY AS YOU GO" basis. This is an encouraging sign but we are not convinced it is legitimate because they still are attempting to collect large fees in advance. If Aussie Air is really going to work on a "pay as you go" basis then why do they still attempt to collect these large fees in advance?

Make sure that you do not deposit more than $2500, at any time, to any flight school including Aussie Air, Inc.

AUSSIE AIR CLOSED IN DAYTONA BEACH

As of August 07, 2009, it does not appear that Aussie Air has any planes in Ft Lauderdale and we expect it is going to be difficult to run a flight school without planes.

Are you a present or former student of Aussie Air?

If you are a present or former student at Aussie Air, we would like to hear from you. We would like to know if you finished your ratings within the advertised time and budget.

Please write us at: jetustudent@gmail.com

Information of Aussie Air

Aussie Air, Inc was started and incorporated August 16, 2004, by a gentleman named, Elia Golfin who is half Greek and Half Australian. In five (5) short years, Mr. Golfin and Aussie Air, Inc have racked up quite a flight school record.

Elia Golfin has been involved in a number of failed Florida flight schools since 2002. Students have lost hundreds of thousands of dollars in Elia Golfin's flight schools.

Elia Golfin also started ASIAUSA LLC on 4/26/2006. Within a short period of time students that had paid for their training, in advance, were having trouble receiving what they had paid for.

FLIGHT SCHOOL STUDENTS COMPLAIN OVER CLOSING

This flight school closing made the Fox channel 9 television news:

FLIGHT SCHOOL CLOSES IN DELAND--STUDENTS LOSE TENS OF THOUSANDS

AsiaUSA had a website before they went out of business and took the students money: You can find it in the wayback machine on Google.

VANESSA PENALVER VS. ASIAUSA,LLC AND ELIA GOLFIN

On September 19, 2008, an employee of AsiaUSA, LLC filed a Fair Labor Standards Act action against AsiaUSA, LLC and Elia Golfin.

4 BUSINESSMEN BOOKED FOR FRAUD

In July 2008 at Chandigarh India, Elia Golfin and three others involved in AsiaUSA were charged with fraud resulting from an Indian student paying for flight training and not receiving that flight training or a refund.

The Better Business Bureau gave AsiaUSA, LLC an "F" rating.

AUSSIE AIR CRASH--STUDENT AND INSTRUCTOR KILLED

There was an Aussie Air plane crash on 11/01/2006. The plane was a Beech Duchess. The Aussie Air student and the instructor were killed.

The NTSB determined the probable cause to be fuel exhaustion. They simply ran out of fuel.

This is the only FATAL crash of a Beech Duchess in the State of Florida since the NTSB started keeping records in 1962. It is only one of two fatal crashes, due to fuel exhaustion, in the entire US in this type aircraft since the NTSB started keeping records in 1962.

The NTSB said that the operator records (Aussie Air) were incomplete. Aussie Air Crash N6017U

The Better Business Bureau also gave Aussie Air, Inc an "F" rating.

Do you still want to do business with this outfit?

ELIA GOLFIN HAS LEFT A TRAIL OF FAILED BUSINESSES IN FLORIDA

Here is a list of Florida Flight Schools and other businesses that Elia Golfin has been involved with in the state of Florida:

AUSSIE AIR, INC
ASIAUSA LLC
BEN AIRCRAFT LEASING LLC
CUBE DESIGN AIRCRAFT LEASING LLC
MARK AIRCRAFT LEASING LLC
ALISON AIRCRAFT LEASING LLC
NEWCASTLE AIRCRAFT LEASING LLC
DELAND NURSING SCHOOL LLC
CAE AVIATION INTERNATIONAL INC.
THE PILOT TRAINING ACADEMY FLORIDA, INC.
TRANS ATLANTIC HOLDING SERVICES INC.
ATLANTIC SHORE ENTERPEISES INC.
THE ISIS MEDIA CORPORATION
WORLD CONTINENTAL, INC.
AUSSIE WIND INC

Here are the results of those businesses from the State of Florida:

AUSSIE AIR, INC was incorporated on 08/16/2004 by Elia Golfin. In 2007 The State of Florida dissolved AUSSIE AIR, INC. On 10/01/2007 the President of AUSSIE AIR, INC., Luis Osvaldo Vargas Martinez applied for reinstatement of the corporation.

ASIAUSA LLC was incorporated on 04/26/2006 and then closed sometime in 2008. Students lost money and 4 people were charged with Fraud.

BEN AIRCRAFT LEASING LLC was incorporated on 09/10/07 and dissolved by the State of Florida on 09/26/08

CUBE DESIGN AIRCRAFT LEASING LLC was incorporated on 09/10/07 and dissolved by the State of Florida on 09/26/08

MARK AIRCRAFT LEASING LLC was incorporated on 09/10/07 and dissolved by the State of Florida on 09/26/08.

ALISON AIRCRAFT LEASING LLC was incorporated on 09/10/07 and dissolved by the State of Florida on 09/26/08

NEWCASTLE AIRCRAFT LEASING LLC was incorporated on 09/10/07 and dissolved by the State of Florida on 09/26/08.

DELAND NURSING SCHOOL LLC was incorporated on 02/12/2008 and the Manager, Ravinder K Gupta resigned on 02/12/2008. A new Manager was not appointed.

CAE AVIATION INTERNATIONAL, INC was incorporated on 11/01/02. Elia Golfin was a director. The Company dissolved 03/19/2004

THE PILOT TRAINING ACADEMY FLORIDA, INC. was incorporated on 11/05/2003. Elia Golfin was Vice President. The company dissolved on 03/19/2004.

TRANS ATLANTIC HOLDING SERVICES INC was incorporated on 12/03/2003. Elia Golfin was Vice President. The company was dissolved by the State of Florida on 10/01/2004.

ATLANTIC SHORE ENTERPEISES INC. was incorporated on 12/03/2003. Elia Golfin was Vice President. The company was dissolved by the State of Florida on 10/01/2004.

THE ISIS MEDIA CORPORATION was incorporated on 03/02/2004. Elia Golfin was Vice President. The company was dissolved on 03/19/2005.

WORLD CONTINENTAL, INC. was incorporated on 11/03/2004. Elia Golfin was the incorporator and Director. The company was dissolved by the State of Florida on 09/16/2005.

AUSSIE WIND INC was incorporated on 09/12/2008. Elia Golfin is the President.

Graduates of Aussie Air

On Aussie Air's website they do list some student graduates. We are concerned about the number of successful graduates at Aussie Air. This school has been in business for five (5) years and there should be about 300 graduates. So far Aussie Air has only listed six (6) graduates 6 on their website and not all of those six (6) have received all of their ratings. Our concern is that there may be a very high flunk out rate at this flight school.

We checked with FAA to see when the "advertised" students did receive their FAA Private, Instrument and Multi Engine ratings as the Aussie Air website says they did.

We were able to confirm that Juan Jose Quiros Jimenez received his Commercial Pilots License on 04/15/2009. He obtained his First Class Medical in 01/08.

Pablo Rodriquez Chaoui received his Commercial Pilots License on 05/25/2009. He obtained his First Class Medical in 01/08.

It appears that it took these students between 400-450 days to obtain their ratings at Aussie Air. That is substantially more time (could be more than twice as much time) than the 210 days listed in Aussie Air's time line. Keep in mind that the longer you are in training--the more it is going to cost you in dorm rent, meals, flight time, flight instruction, etc.

According to sources, Aussie Air will quote a prospective student a training cost of $50,000 for all of their ratings. Aussie Air does expect to add extra charges to this initial quotation and the total cost of the Aussie Air training could run $125,000.00.

We are also being told that Aussie Air will not let students fly until they are VERY PROFICIENT in English. So you could arrive in the US, and spend many months learning English before you will be allowed to fly. This may be one of the reasons that the training is taking so much longer than the Aussie air advertisement represents.

Two graduates listed on the site that took 400-450 days to receive their license from the time they received their student pilot and/or medical certificate:

Juan José Quiros & Pablo Rodriguez Chaoui
(2,008)

Granada, Spain
(PPL-FAA; IR-FAA; CPL-FAA; ME-FAA)
Juan Francisco Marti
PPL-FAA; IR-FAA

Juan received his First Class Medical in January 2008. He received his instrument rating on 05/17/2009. It would appear that it has taken Juan over 400 days to receive his Private and Instrument rating. That is substantially more time than the 120 days that Aussie Air advertises in their time line

Rodrigo Mestre Galofre
PPL-FAA; IR-FAA

Rodrigo received his First Class Medical in August 2008. He received his instrument rating on 04/03/09.
It would appear that it has taken Rodrigo over 210 days to receive his Private and Instrument rating. This is more time than the 120 days that Aussie Air advertises in their time line.

WE ARE HAVING TROUBLE FINDING STUDENTS THAT COMPLETED THEIR TRAINING AT AUSSIE AIR ON TIME AND AS PROMISED

If you are a present or former student at Aussie Air, then we would like to talk with you. Please contact us at: jetustudent@gmail.com. We will keep your identity confidential.

Because we are having trouble verifying that Aussie Air can actually deliver what they promise and advertise to most of their students, then we have some STRONG recommendations for any prospective student considering going to Aussie Air or any flight school:

1. UNDER NO CIRCUMSTANCES PAY MORE THAN $2500 IN ADVANCE, TO ANY FLIGHT SCHOOL, FOR ANY REASON AT ANYTIME. No matter how good they make it sound. No matter what discount they offer, PAY AS YOU GO. Do not have more than $2500 on deposit at anytime. It is better to NOT take the discount than to LOSE the ENTIRE AMOUNT and not get your training.

2. READ RULE ONE AND MAKE SURE YOU DO NOT BREAK IT!

3. Make sure Aussie Air has the proper insurance BEFORE you give them any money. If Aussie Air does not have the proper insurance and you have an accident then YOU can be sued and possibly lose everything you have. Here is the insurance Aussie Air should have:

a. LIABILITY INSURANCE

B. ERRORS AND OMISSIONS INSURANCE

C. WORKMAN'S COMP INSURANCE

D. CONTENT INSURANCE and PROPERTY INSURANCE

If Aussie Air does not have these insurance coverages then do not go to this school! Companies that don't have the proper insurances are often deficient in other areas as well. Do not take a chance. The school should be able to provide you with a certificate of insurance showing these coverages.

4. Talk to at least 3 students that went to Aussie Air and received what they had paid for. Ask questions such as how long it took?, any delays?, were the planes available?, Were the instructors available?

5. Beware of EXTRA CHARGES. In looking over the Aussie Air website they have a lot of areas that indicate EXTRA CHARGES are going to be added. Most of their programs are quoted at minimum times. Most students can not complete flight training with the FAA minimum times. When you go over the minimum times you are going to be charged extra. This can double or triple the cost of your training or you can run out of money and not be able to finish your training. Ask the former students about these EXTRA CHARGES.

AUSSIE AIR AIRCRAFT FLEET

If you go to the Aussie Air website you will find the following planes listed as being part of the training fleet:

N94945 1983 CESSNA 152 (CERTIFICATE TERMINATED BY THE FAA)

This aircraft;s registration status may not be suitable for operation. Please contact the Aircraft Registration Branch at 1-866-09434 for additional information.

N64848 1978 CESSNA 152

N965AA 1978 CESSNA 152

N68197 1978 CESSNA 152

N2208E 1979 CESSNA 172N (CERTIFICATE TERMINATED BY THE FAA)

This aircraft;s registration status may not be suitable for operation. Please contact the Aircraft Registration Branch at 1-866-09434 for additional information.

N5456D 1979 CESSNA 172N

N7420J 1968 PIPER ARROW

N1859U 2005 CESSNA 172SP (OUT OF FLEET)

N6013M BEECHCRAFT DUTCHESS

The pictures and website links have been removed, from this section, for this published book version.

Chapter Five

HOW THE BIG SCAM WORKS

This is the heart of this book. It's the censored information about how the advance payment flight training scam works. This scam has probably been going on since before you were born.

The previous chapter on Aussie Air demonstrated what happens to a flight school student after they pay their tuition money upfront.

This chapter shows you how the bad guys create and run the scam.

The Flight Training Industry in the United States is broken. Literally ANYONE can set up a flight school in short order by renting a plane, hiring an instructor and running advertisements.

No experience is necessary to open a flight school. You don't have to be a pilot or even have a pilot's license to open a flight school.

You don't even need money to open a flight school because there is absolutely NO REGULATION of flight schools in most states including Florida, Arizona and Texas where most flight schools are located.

California has now included flight schools under regulation of the Bureau of Private Secondary Schools in Sacramento effective May 17, 2010

You don't need insurance to open a flight school. You don't need to be bonded to open a flight school.

You can get out of jail one day and open a flight school the next day and there is nothing that anyone can do to stop it.

You can then start charging students, $50,000, $75,000 or $100,000, or more, up front for flight training the very same day.

You can collect the money from the student one day and spend all of the money on a trip to Vegas, a new car, new house, new furniture or for any other reason. Nobody will stop you.

It doesn't matter because there is no regulation requiring you to safeguard the money, that the student has paid you, for flight training.

When the student actually wants and expects his flight training you can refuse to give it to him and the student is now stuck with hiring an attorney that will not be able to get his money back since the school has no assets.

A bad flight school can lease a plane, string the owner of the plane along and not pay for the plane. The owner will eventually repossess the plane after the flight school has not paid for the plane.

This usually takes several months. Meanwhile the flight school has had use of the plane and not paid for it. The flight school will simply get more planes from other owners that are too lazy to check the flight school out and not pay those owners and keep the process going.

It's one of the easiest businesses to get into because MOST STATES have exempted Flight Schools from any sort of licensing or regulation.

THERE ARE A LOT OF BAD FLIGHT SCHOOLS

The bad flight schools are bad for Aviation. They are bad for the industry. They are bad for the good legitimate flight schools that have to compete with these bad schools.

Until the industry really gets their act together and demands proper regulation of this industry, we are doomed to continue with the same results.

Even the good flight schools have a conflict here. In order to compete with the scam flight schools that advertise an unrealistic price for training that they can not possibly provide, the legitimate school is forced to advertise a price based on FAA minimum hours.

Most pilots will not finish their ratings in the minimum hours. It actually takes almost twice the FAA minimum hours for most Private Pilots to obtain their license. Who pays for this extra time? The student does of course.

There is no incentive for a flight school to finish up a student quickly. This is because the faster they finish up the student--- THE LESS MONEY the flight school makes.

What is the incentive for finishing up the student fast? Less money?

THE FAA DOES NOT REGULATE FLIGHT SCHOOLS

The FAA does not regulate flight schools. Even if the FAA discovers that a Flight School is breaking some law or regulation--the FAA is powerless to do anything about it. Flight Schools do not come under the jurisdiction of the FAA. The FAA has never evaluated a financial statement of any Flight School. The FAA has never required any sort of financial responsibility or financial requirement from a flight school. The FAA does not get involved in any consumer issues or consumer protection issues.

MOST STUDENT PILOTS NEVER RECEIVE THEIR PILOTS LICENSE

OVER 63% OF THE STUDENT PILOTS NEVER RECEIVE THEIR PILOTS LICENSE!

That is what we call a "wash out rate".

In 2008 the FAA issued 61,194 Student Pilot Certificates. Yet only 19,052 Private Pilot Licenses were granted. The wash out rate in 2008 was 63%. Only 37% of the students actually received their Private Pilot License.

In 2007 the FAA issued 66,953 Student Pilot Certificates. Yet only 20,299 Private Pilot Licenses were granted. The wash out rate in 2007 was 64%. Only 36% of the students actually received their Private Pilots License.

My "friends" at AOPA have informed me that the WASH OUT RATE is actually higher than 62%. It may actually be as high as 82%.

The reason for this is because a student pilot does not usually obtain a student pilot certificate until just before he or she is ready to solo.

So a student pilot can take 9 or more flying lessons without obtaining a student pilot certificate. Since the FAA has no record of those students, they can not be included in the FAA numbers listed above.

Can you imagine that 82 out of 100 flight school students wash out and do not even obtain their Private Pilots License?

If that does not convince you not to prepay for in advance for your flight training; then nothing will!

To put this another way, the odds are stacked against the student pilot.

Do you think that the flight schools that collect the money upfront know this BIG DIRTY SECRET?

Of course they do.

Has anyone ever told you this information before? Of course not. They want to keep you in the dark. Knowledge is power. When you don't have the knowledge you will pay more.

Once you pay your money you have a very slim chance of getting the money back even if you can't finish the course or obtain your license.

Massive CANCELLATION FEES and NON REFUNDABLE DEPOSITS insure the deck is stacked against the student pilot.

We know of an early Jet University Sim Center student that paid $30,000 up front for his training. He entered the flight school ground class. He was in the class room for only 4 weeks. He never flew a plane. He was kicked out of class for failing a stage test. The school kept $19,000 for the four weeks of classroom training.

WHY DO STUDENTS WASH OUT?

There are a number of reasons that a student pilot will wash out of the system:

1. The course is too difficult for them. Not everyone can be a pilot. A pilot must be able to multi-task.

2. Time Constraints. Flight training, like most things takes longer than you expect.

3. Money. Students run out of money. Flight training can cost 2-3 times the amount quoted by a flight school.

4. Flight training is not what they expected. Flight training is not a video or simulator game. It's serious business. Although it can be a lot of fun, it can also be quite uncomfortable at times.

5. Family issues. Wives, girlfriends, husbands, boyfriends, kids and parents often find it difficult for a student pilot to be away. This may put additional pressure on the student pilot.

6. Job Issues. It's often difficult to find time to pursue aviation when you are holding down a job.

7. Weather Issues. A student pilot can't fly when the weather is bad.

8. The training may be inadequate. Since there is no standard training program within the aviation industry, instruction, course content and presentation does vary.

9. The flight school may try to wash you out on purpose. If you have paid a large amount up front and your contract calls for cancellation fees; a flight school may try to wash you out on purpose so they can keep your money!

They do this by convincing you that you don't study hard enough, you don't take this serious, you don't speak English well enough, you are a bad pilot and will never make it at an airline as well as any number of "trumped up" reasons. The end result is that students leave, do not receive their training and the flight school keeps the money.

BEWARE OF THE HIDDEN TRAPS

There are some flight schools that will do everything possible to "reel you in" and get you to sign an expensive flight school contract.

These types of schools have sales departments that will stay in constant contact with you until you sign the contract and pay your money. They will make everything sound great.

They may show you pictures of luxury apartments that you will be staying in. They may represent a lot of things to get you to fork over your money.

Things will change once you arrive at the flight school for your training. The flight school will now do everything possible to keep you from flying.

The most common delay tactic is to put you in a ground school class. Ground school classes are cheap and they don't cost the flight school much at all. A flight school will have every excuse in the world why you need to stay in ground school before you fly. And that is where you will stay for a while.

When you finally figure out what is going on, they will start to put you in an aircraft. Months could have passed. They have broken you down much like a high pressure car dealership does when you are buying a car.

At this point you are so happy to actually be able to fly that you won't realize that you are not flying much at all. The "fight school trick" seems to be to allow you to fly 4-5 hours during the first flying month just to keep you strung along.

The flight school will then claim you are not making progress. They will claim you are a slow student. They will say you should study harder. They will tell you that need to be more serious about your career.

Of course, this is all not true. The fact is that the flight school slowed you down. It's all part of the process. It's designed to break you down and finally for you to give up. It's designed to get you to leave the flight school.

These types of flight schools are designed to get you to quit, flunk out or just leave. When you leave, the flight school will keep your money and you will not get it back.

SILVER STATE HELICOPTERS is an example of a flight school that used these deceptive methods and then went out of business leaving over 2000 students without their flight training:

You must understand that once you pay the flight school a large sum of money in advance then they usually spend it very quickly. The money is not held in a trust account. It's simply gone.

You have now put the flight school in a position of COSTING THEM MONEY for every service you use. It doesn't matter that you paid for all of these services in advance. So the flight school has an incentive to get rid of you. If they can get rid of you then you will not cost them any more money.

Want to avoid this?

DO NOT PAY ANY FLIGHT SCHOOL ANY MORE THAN $2500 IN ADVANCE FOR ANY REASON. DO NOT LET A FLIGHT SCHOOL GET AHEAD OF YOU BY MORE THAN $2500 EVER!

If everyone would follow this advice then students will not lose money. Flight schools will have to be properly capitalized and the whole industry will benefit.

WHAT SHOULD YOU DO IF YOU HAVE BEEN RIPPED OFF BY A FLIGHT SCHOOL?

The very first thing you should do if you have been ripped off by a flight school is to file a report with the BETTER BUSINESS BUREAU.

You can file a complaint online by going to www.bbb.org.

Although filing a report with the BBB may not get your money back, it does create a permanent record of a complaint for the flight school. When potential students look at the BBB website then it will show any record of past problems. It will also indicate how the flight school solved the problem. Maybe the school will be persuaded to make things right to avoid future problems.

Also, if students actually do start filing BBB complaints, it may cause that school to 'shape up" its business practices.

A flight school will not be able to stay in business with a whole stack of unresolved BBB complaints.

FILE A COMPLAINT WITH JETUNIVERSITYSUCKS.COM

Our student volunteers will look at your case and help guide you through the process.

We will contact your school and attempt to persuade them to work out a fair solution for you and for them.

To file a case with us, please write to: jetustudent@gmail.com and include your contact information as well as information about your case. We will need to speak with you by telephone.

YOU CAN FILE SUIT IN SMALL CLAIMS COURT

If you have followed our advice and not let the flight school get more than $2500 ahead of you, and you have not received your training then you can file an action in small claims court.

Small claims has a limit on the amount you can sue for. Each state sets it's own limit. That's why it's called small claims court! Most areas are $5000 or less. You will need to check with your local clerk of court to determine the limit in the county where your flight school is located.

If you watch Judge Judy or The Peoples Court you get a great insight into how small claims court works. There are not attorneys. You represent yourself and present your evidence.

If you have your facts and paperwork together then you will probably win. If you are disorganized and don't have your facts and case in order then you will lose even if you should have won. Make sure you have your paperwork, e-mails, evidence, witnesses, etc all in court on the date of your small claims trial.

A judge will decide if you are owed the money and issue a judgment against the flight school if you are successful. If the school wants to stay in business then they will have to pay you.

The cost to file a small claims case is usually less than $200 and you obtain the forms from your local clerk of courts office. If you win the case, then the costs are added to the judgment and the flight school will have to pay those costs as well.

Chapter Six

The Fake Scholarship

This information was censored by WEBS.com

This was an interesting last ditch effort that Jet University came up with as they were going down. I'm sure it's been done before. We have had some recent e-mails lately about a firm in Delaware that is doing the same thing. It really didn't work very well at Jet University because we detailed how it worked on the student website.

Here is how the marketing program works. The school sets up a fake Airline Pilot Training Association and will put out a press release indicating that scholarships are available for flight training. Since pilot training is so expensive, this is attractive to a student pilot.

The press release will be picked up by the AOPA and NATA magazines as well as other news outlets.

The student fills out a scholarship application and it is faxed back to a phone number which happens to be the sales department at the flight school.

The next thing that happens is that the student gets a call and is informed that they have received his scholarship application and it is being reviewed by the scholarship committee.

They are calling to make sure he is still interested because there are many people competing for the scholarship and they want to make sure he would be able to come to the school by a certain date if he were fortunate enough to win the (fake) scholarship. If he can't come they want to be able to offer the scholarship to someone that really can use it.

This is nothing more than a qualifying call to make sure the applicant will be able to come up with $15,000 (or more) for his "contribution" to the scholarship.

The sales department will then string the scholarship applicant along for a few more days and get him excited about winning a scholarship.

The (sales) representative will tell the applicant that the committee will have a decision by Friday.

When Friday comes, the student will not have heard anything and he will call the representative back. The representative will tell the applicant that something came up and the committee could not meet today. They will meet on Monday.

This is all designed to keep an applicant excited over the weekend.

Finally on Monday, the applicant will receive the good news that he has "won" a scholarship from the flight school. What the student does not know is that everyone wins a scholarship from the flight school as long as they are willing to pay thousands of dollars in advance.

Now the flight school will attempt to collect the student contribution for his part of the scholarship in advance. The student is so excited and does not realize he is being scammed.

He will do everything in his power to come up with the $15,000 or more so he can take advantage of the scholarship.

If you run across something like this, remember the rule.

DO NOT PAY ANY FLIGHT SCHOOL MORE THAN $2500 IN ADVANCE FOR ANY REASON NO MATTER HOW GOOD THEY MAKE IT SOUND.

Chapter Seven

TIPS TO SAVE YOU MONEY

If I have saved one student pilot from getting ripped off then this book is a success. One thing that I have learned in my lifetime is the less you know about something—the more you are going to pay for it.

Of course there is nothing wrong with that as long as you get what you pay for. This is America and this is a capitalistic economy. The problem comes when you pay for something and do not receive what you pay for.

Aviation is expensive at any level. It is hard for anyone to make legitimate money in aviation. Planes are expensive. Maintenance is expensive. Fuel is expensive. There just are not any real easy legitimate shortcuts to cut costs.

The bad guys in flight training industry have found a way to cut costs. It's not a legitimate way, but they do it. They simply collect large amounts of money up front from students for flight training and then do not provide that training for one reason or another.

The bad guys know that over 63% of the students are pretty much guaranteed to wash out. If you are one of the 63% that washes out, (you have better than a 6 in 10 chance of being one that washes out) you are not going to get the money, you paid in advance, back.

The best way to avoid this is to not pay in advance for any flight training.

Most flight schools do not charge in advance for anything other than a flight kit which you are going to need. A flight kit might run $200-$400 and will contain the books and other media materials you need for your studies. My advice is to not buy the flight kit until after your third lesson.

Once you have had three lessons, you will figure out if you want to continue. It's OK to make the investment in the flight kit at that point because you have demonstrated that you can go up and come back down without getting sick or getting dizzy. Most people don't have this problem, but what if you did?

I will always suggest that you obtain your Private Pilot training at a local airport near where you are right now. I learned to fly at a large airport near where I live. That gave me to confidence to get in and out of any airport large or small. If you can find a medium or large airport near you that has flight training then it will serve you well.

I have seen some issues where students learn to fly at a small uncontrolled field and they don't learn the basics to properly get in and out of a large controlled airport.

It's not to say you can't learn at a small field. But if you are looking to be a professional pilot, it is my personal opinion that you will learn better at a controlled airfield with a tower.

Don't rush your training. The minimum number of hours required to obtain a Private Pilots license is 40. However the average number of hours that a Private Pilot has when he tests for his license is 60-75 hours.

You will not hurt yourself by getting more hours while you are training to be a Private Pilot. All of those hours count towards your future ratings and those private pilot hours are going to be the cheapest ones you ever have. If you have 100 hours when you get your private then you will just need 150 more before you get your commercial.

Once you get that private ticket, go out and enjoy it. Rack up some nice cross country VFR hours. All of that will count towards your commercial rating. You won't have to "time build" as much later.

When I was in flight school, there were many students flying all over Florida bored out of their minds "time building" just to get the 250 hours necessary for a commercial rating. Some of these students needed 100 hours of boring time building. It gets old really fast and it gets expensive really fast as well. 100 hours of time building will cost you at least $15,000 these days.

I had my hours and I didn't have to time build. I got those hours while I was a Private Pilot. They were cheaper hours and I promise you that I had a much better time obtaining those hours flying my friends around. You can also get in some of your long cross countries that you need in your logbook for your commercial rating while you have your private rating. If you do them now, then you don't have to do them later. Talk to your flight instructor about this after you get your private so that you know exactly what you need.

The other place you can spend some extra time on is during your instrument rating. This will be the most important rating you will get and any extra time spent on this rating is not wasted. All of the hours count towards your commercial rating.

Some have asked me if you should ever pay in advance. I would prefer than you not ever pay in advance for flight training.

However there are some legitimate exceptions that might require a pre-payment. These exceptions involve reserving a plane or a specific piece of equipment like a jet simulator. If you reserve something and the equipment can't be rented to someone else then you will sometimes be asked to pay in advance.

No matter what, that pre-payment should never exceed $2500 tops. You should always try to do it for less. $2500 is the maximum. That is enough to show you are serious. Also the bad guys won't try to scam you for $2500 because they can't make enough doing it. If for some reason you don't get what you paid for then you can always go to small claims court. This limits your risk.

If you can book directly with an independent flight instructor then you will have a wonderful experience and you will probably save some money. The flight instructor may have a plane. If he doesn't then he is going to know the best place in the area to rent one.

To find an independent flight instructor, you can ask your friends that fly, look on Craig's List or call a local member of the Civil Air Patrol for a recommendation. The Civil Air Patrol people know where the flight instructors are.

Don't be afraid to change flight instructors if things are not working out for you. Sometimes you just can't click with someone for one reason or another.

If you are having trouble then switch to another instructor and see if that helps solve the problem. Flight instructors understand this. I learn better with some instructors. I always seem to do better with the more experienced instructors. But that is just me. You should do what works best for you.

There is another way to save some money on flight training if you weigh less than 195 pounds!

There are some older workhouse Cessna 150's and 152's still around. Most are probably older than you are. Although these aircraft have some age on them; they still fly the same and have been used as trainers for many years. They are all steam gauge aircraft. There is not a glass cockpit in any of them!

These older Cessna aircraft can usually be rented for $65-$85 per hour. This can save you up to $100 an hour over the newer aircraft. So if you don't weigh more than 195 pounds, this might be an option for you.

Chapter Eight

Costs and How to Pay For Your Flight Training

As you begin your flight training, you will no doubt want to know how much this is going to cost before you get done.

Since there is no standard flight training program it is going to be just about impossible for someone to quote you an exact cost. Just keep in mind that whatever someone quotes you will always be on the low end. It will almost always cost more than you think.

Most schools will quote FAA minimums. Most students take up to twice what the minimums specify. Remember the minimums are just minimums that the FAA requires.

Most people are not proficient at the minimums and the FAA also requires that you be proficient before they let you fly around the sky in a flying machine.

What I suggest you do is break down your training into modules and break out the expenses so that you can understand where those expenses come from.

Here are the direct expenses that you will incur during your flight training:

1. Books, Charts and Training Materials
2. Headphone and i Pad Costs
3. Rental of Aircraft or Simulator
4. Flight Instructor Fees
5. Ground Instructor Fees
6. Fuel Cost
7. FAA Examination Fees for License and Medical.

Let's examine these costs a bit so you can better understand them.

1. Books, Charts and Training Materials. Many schools have a flight kit available for purchase which includes a couple of books, some navigation aids, workbooks and possibly some videos. This will cost you $200-$400 for each rating. You buy them one rating at a time. You should buy the Private Pilot Kit after you have completed your third flight lesson.
2. Headphones and iPad Cost. You will not need these for your first few lessons. The rental planes have headphones. I would wait a bit on these items, but you are going to want to get them before you solo. A good set of Bose Aviation Noise Reduction Headphones will run about $1100 if you can swing

it. The Noise Reduction Headphones protect your hearing and are worth the extra expense. You already know how much iPads cost. iPads are now an important part of aviation and you need to be familiar with their flight applications.
3. Rental of Aircraft or simulator. You are going to need an aircraft to train in. You will rent a single engine aircraft. Single engine plane rental rates will run between $100-$200 per air hour depending on which one you rent. Some aircraft are rented "wet" (with fuel) and some are rented "dry" (without fuel) Virtually all aircraft manufacturers only make glass cockpit aircraft these days and you will need to train in one of those aircraft for most of your training. In the beginning you might rent an older "steam gauge aircraft. My recommendation is that you get in the glass cockpit aircraft as quickly as possible. All airlines fly with glass cockpits and this is what you are going to be flying for most of your life. If you become a flight instructor you might spend several hundred hours teaching in some older non glass cockpit aircraft, but those will be going away simply because they don't make them anymore. A general aviation simulator rents for $35-$85 per hour depending on the model. I really have been impressed with the Redbird simulators.
4. Flight Instructor fees will vary between $35-$100 per air hour depending on where you obtain your flight training. Expect to pay on the higher end of the scale at the places that advertise a lot. Some schools will charge a fee for the instructor in addition to the air hour for the pre and post flight

briefings. You will need to know if your school does this so that you can properly budget.

5. Ground instructor fees should be less than Flight Instructor fees. You will need to know how much your school charges for ground instruction. Some schools do not do much (if any) ground instruction and you won't have a charge. They simply will tell you to get a set videos and prep for the written test on your own. Some will have a formal class that you need to attend for ground instruction. Ground instruction can run from $8 to $50 an hour depending on class size and facility.

6. Fuel costs keep going up. A single engine aircraft burns between 9-12 gallons of fuel per air hour depending on the model. Aviation fuel cost is about $6.40 a gallon as I write this. If you burn 10 gallons an hour you are going to spend $64.00 per hour on fuel. Remember you are going to need a minimum of 250 hours to get your commercial pilots license. That's going to cost you almost $20,000 in fuel costs.

7. FAA examination fees. There are two per rating that you will need to pay. The written test fee is currently $150. The aircraft check ride is $250-$500 depending on the FAA designated pilot examiner. Each designated pilot examiner sets his own fee. The DPE is not an FAA employee. Most people do not know that you can have an FAA inspector employee do your aircraft check ride at no charge. You would need to set an appointment with the local FSBO office to be able to do this. Sometimes it takes

a long time to get an appointment and sometimes you can get one right away.

8. You will also need a FAA medical examination and you will need to go to an FAA DME for this. Medical examinations come in three "types" First Class, Second Class and Third Class. The most extensive (and most expensive) is the First Class medical which is what you would need to fly for the airlines. When you are just starting out all you need is a third class medical. When you complete your first medical, the doctor will also issue you a student pilot certificate. Medicals will run from $65-$250 depending on who you go to and what type you need. There are some that believe that if you intend to be a professional pilot then you should apply for a First Class Medical at the beginning of your training so that you can "make sure" that you qualify for a First Class Medical. You don't want to spend tens of thousands of dollars, on flight training, and get to the end and find out you can not qualify for a First Class Medical. If you know you want to be a commercial pilot then I would agree that you should apply for the First Class Medical at the beginning just to make sure everything is OK. You will not need to get another medical for several years because your First Class Medical will automatically change to a Second Class and then a Third Class after a period of time. Your fight instructor will tell you more about this. This section will also be covered on your FAA written test!

I have broken out the costs above. Most schools will bundle some of the costs together. However you do need to know how all of this works.

How do you pay for your flight training?

As you can see from the numbers above, flight training is very expensive. By the time you get to your commercial pilot certificate you are going to spend tens of thousands of dollars

. You need a minimum of 250 flight hours. On the low end that is going to cost you $200 per air hour and that is $50,000. That only includes the cost of the aircraft and instructor.

To that you have to add extra hours, extra instruction, training materials, examination fees and all of the other items you will need.

The best way to budget this is to start at the beginning.

Start with your Private and work the budget out. Today, I would budget $15,000 for your Private. Figure it will take you 6-9 months to get your private if you fly part time about 10 hours per month. That will put you in the air about 7 flights per month. That is about two flights a week and that is a pretty good pace so that you are able to absorb what you are learning.

If you are on this schedule then you will need $2000 per month for your flight training. If you have friends or relatives that ask what you want for Christmas or a Birthday; do not be bashful about asking them to buy you a flight lesson or two.

My mother in law asked me what I wanted for Christmas one year and I quickly told her a new set of Bose Aviation Headphones. That's what she gave me! Since I am so "hard to buy for" this was the perfect solution.

BORROWING MONEY FOR FLIGHT TRAINING

Most pilots do not believe in borrowing money for flight training. The reason for this is because when you get to the end you have a $70,000+ debt and you do not have the income to pay back the debt. You will be much better off paying as you go. Make some money and then go fly. Make some more money and fly some more.

There are some pilots that believe that if you do not get a loan, it will take you much longer to complete your training. This can be true. I personally don't recommend getting a loan solely for flight training, but if you have no other way then there is one company that I know of that does provide financing for pilot training.

Pilot Finance, Inc. finances flight training through flight schools that are enrolled to offer their programs. They also hold the money and do not send it the flight school in advance.

They normally will not approve additional financing for more training until you have paid back at least 50% of what you have borrowed already.

Their interest rates are almost what a credit card charges, but if you can make the payments on time and not have any late or missed payments they will rebate you back a good portion of the interest charges. Their website is at:

http://www.pilotfinance.com/

DON'T RUSH YOUR RATINGS

I also need to point out that the FAA never intended that you would get all of your ratings in a short period of time. The FAA intended that you would have each of your ratings for some period of time before moving to another rating. The reason for this is to give you a solid foundation and let you get some real experience flying from which to build upon.

So instead of trying to get your ratings in as short of a time period as possible, I recommend that you pace yourself and spend the time to really get the experience that you need. Do not be in such a hurry!

Sometimes you will see a Part 141 school that will advertise that you can get your ratings in less hours. That is true if everything goes exactly right. It's not so true when things go wrong like failing a stage check.

You can shave almost 60 hours off of your commercial training by going to a Part 141 school. The problem with this method is that you also have 60 hours less flight experience. As a student pilot you need more hours—not less hours. Those 60 lost hours will need to be made up later in order for you to get your ATP.

There is one other way that can make sense if you are really, really serious about flying and know you are going to get all of your ratings. You would only do this after you get your private pilot rating.

Once you have your private pilot rating you have accomplished something that most people will never have. You are to be congratulated because 63% of the people that started their flight training will never accomplish what you have.

So if you are really serious about this, you can look at purchasing an aircraft. There are a couple of reasons for this. When you finish your Private you may have around 100 hours. You are going to need at least another 150 hours to obtain your commercial rating. You are going to need to rent a plane to do those 150 hours. That plane rental is going to cost you a minimum of $22,000.

Since you are going to spend $22,000 anyway renting an aircraft, why not consider purchasing a good used plane for around $40,000 or so and finish up your training in your own aircraft. When you get done training you can sell your aircraft (if you want) and get most (if not all) of your $40,000 back.

You will need to get someone to help you with this that really knows airplanes. A pre-buy inspection is mandatory by a qualified aircraft mechanic. You will need to be fully aware of all of the costs involved like insurance, parking, maintenance, etc.

You might also find another pilot that would be interested in purchasing the plane with you. That way you can split the costs of the aircraft. This would be a win win for both parties.

The great thing about buying a plane is that you can finance the plane and that will help defer some of your training costs and possibly save you some money in the process. This is the only time I will personally recommend that you finance anything related to aviation. Please do make sure you already have your Private Pilot license before you do this.

Chapter Nine

Contracts and Conditions

Most flight schools do not have written contracts. That's because they really do not need them! Most flight schools are pay as you go which means that you pay or swipe your credit card after each flight lesson that you take. It's kind of like going to a restaurant. You sit down and order a meal. When you get finished, you pay the bill. If things are not working out then you can simply stop coming and find another flight school or restaurant.

So with that being said, why do some flight schools have written contracts that look so much like the paperwork you have to sign when buying a car? I'll give you a hint; the flight school contracts are NOT there to protect you!

So if the written contracts are not there to protect the student, then they can only exist for the benefit of the flight school.

A written contract is a legal document and you should never sign any legal document unless you have YOUR attorney review that document.

This is especially true with flight school contracts because they have many many paragraphs of hidden terms and conditions that you are not going to be familiar with.

As I have already told you, over 62% of the people that begin flight training, wash out. They do not even get to first base and obtain their private pilot's license. Although I hope you become a great pilot, you must consider that you may flunk out. You must know what will happen if you do have to leave the flight school.

You can bet that most of these flight school contracts are going to have a massive unfair cancellation penalty that you will be charged if you "break the contract" and flunk out of flight school like most people do. You can bet that the flight school knows every part of their contract and has many different ways to keep your money and not provide your flight training and not return your money.

You can also bet that most of these flight school contracts will have clauses that will allow the school to add extra charges to your bill even if you prepaid for your flight training.

I want you to think about something.

Suppose you want to attend a four year university like most students do when they graduate from high school. What if that university wanted you to pay your entire 4 years of tuition in advance? Would you do it? Do you know anyone that has done it or would do it? Of course not.

If you are going to any four year college you pay the fees a semester at a time. If you leave or flunk out, then you don't pay anymore. That's the way it works. The university will not have massive cancellation policies. The most you could possibly lose would be the money that you paid for that semester.

If you really do grasp this concept then there is no way that it would make any sense to pay a flight school in advance for all of your pilot ratings. It would be just like paying a 4 year university all of the money up front for your degree.

There is absolutely no advantage, to you, in paying for your flight training up front. You can lose every penny you paid in advance and end up with absolutely nothing. Thousands and thousands of flight school students have had this happen to them over the past 30 years. Some never did recover. Some never did become pilots. Some took many years to pay off student loans for ratings they never received.

Some of the flight school contracts have a guaranteed refund policy. It looks good on paper. But when it comes time to get your refund, the school will not pay you. Remember the Aussie Air Chapter? All of those students had a contract that provided for a refund. Yet none of the students was ever able to collect a refund! So the refund guarantee was not worth the paper it was printed on.

Well let's suppose you read everything in this book and you still have SJS (Shiny Jet Syndrome) and those $70,000 flight school academies are just proving so irresistible to you. You like the idea of getting your ratings as quickly as possible. (which is not the greatest idea by the way)

The only way that I would ever recommend that you enroll in one of those programs is if you were able to pay no more than $2500 in advance.

The school is not going to like this arrangement because they can't get their hands on your money and they are going to come up with every excuse why you can not do it.

What you should do is offer to deposit all of the money with your attorney and he will hold that money in his trust account. He will disburse the money to the flight school as it comes due. If the school will not honor this arrangement, then find another school or a local FBO or local CFI.

You must understand why the school does not like this type of arrangement. The pay in advance flight schools are literally banking on 62% (or more) of the students flunking out.

The flight schools make a lot of money on washed out students. If the school can collect $70,000 up front and spend $10,000 getting a student flunked out and then keep the other $60,000 for doing nothing; it becomes a very profitable business.

Chapter Ten

What You Should Consider If You Are Thinking About Flight Training

If you have read though this book, you will notice something if you are paying close attention.

Not one time did I tell you that you should not do this. Not one time this I try to discourage you from entering this profession.

What I have tried to do throughout this book is make you aware of the scams and rip offs in this industry. This is so you will be able to identify the red flags when you see them.

A few bad guys in the flight training industry does not make this a bad industry. After all there are bad guys in every industry and profession.

Red flags should go up as soon as someone asks you to pay more than $2500 in advance for flight training. That is the biggest clue you will come across. That is when you need to walk away and find another flight school. Just say no.

If you will do that then you will never have an issue where you lose money on flight training.

So let's say you really get it. You are never going to pay some flight school more than $2500 upfront because you know better. What is the first step and when should you take it?

The FAA does not have an age limitation on when you can begin flight training. You can start training, at any age, as soon as you are capable. My daughter started her flight lessons when she was 12.

The reason that you can start flight training at any age is because flying is pretty safe. Some claim it's more safe than driving a car.

Although you can start flight training at any age, you can not solo until your 16th birthday. So if you are under 16, you are going to have a flight instructor sitting next to you on each and every flight. That's a good thing!

The flight instructor does not have to touch the controls if you can fly the plane. However the instructor is trained to take over the controls if he needs to.

Instructors will not turn the controls over to you until you are ready. On your very first lesson, you will actually fly and control the plane for much of the flight. Your instructor will probably want to land the plane on the first flight, but he will demonstrate, to you, how it is done.

So the question is, when should you begin your training? The answer to that question is simple. You begin when you are ready and have the time and funds to do it.

Fourteen is probably as good an age as any to begin. You probably have a lot of free time that you can devote to flight training. But if you want to wait until later, then that is OK as well. Just set your goals and pace yourself. Try to fly at least 2-3 times a month if you have the resources available.

How cool would it be to be able to solo on your 16th birthday and obtain your Private Pilot's License on your 17th birthday?

HOW TO GET STARTED FLYING

To get started, you are going to need to sign up for a discovery flight at a local flight training facility. Discovery flights are introductory flights that every flight school (or instructor) has. It is usually your first flight lesson.

The first flight lesson is usually sold at a reduced cost to get you interested. The flight schools generally do not make money on discovery flights. They take you up as a form of advertising (one time) with the hope that you will become a regular customer and sign up for flight lessons at their flight school.

On the discovery flight you will actually get to fly the plane and feel what it is like to be a real pilot. **All pilots started with a discovery flight, just like you, no matter what kind of aircraft or spaceship they later flew in their careers!**

WHAT KIND OF PLANE WILL YOU BE FLYING?

All flight schools (big and small) have pretty much the same types of planes for training students. You might be flying a single engine 2 passenger (you and the instructor) training aircraft such as a Cessna 150, 152 or a Diamond DA20. Some schools will put you in a single engine 4 seat Piper Cherokee, Cessna 172 or Diamond DA40.

The reason that I am listing these planes is because you might think that if you spend $70,000 at one of those large prepaid tuition schools, that you will be flying different aircraft. You won't be. You will generally be flying the same types of planes no matter where you do your training. Some may be older than others, but that is going to be the extent of it.

Although those large schools will show you pictures of jets, you will not fly a real jet until you get all of your ratings. Most pilots do not get to fly a real jet until they have been hired by the airlines and they are actually flying airline passengers. That will be many years from now. Up until that point, a pilots jet time is limited to the simulators in most cases.

The exception to this rule is if you get hired as a corporate pilot or if you obtain advanced training (after you get your ratings) at one of the few advanced training facilities that actually have jets. I know of two in the US. I attended one of them in Ohio.

THE CIVIL AIR PATROL

If you are under 20 and you are considering a career in aviation, you should check into joining the Civil Air Patrol as a cadet. You will be serving your country with other teens that are interested in the same things that you are. You can join when you are 12 and this is a great program for teens. It does not cost much, but does require a time commitment. You can find out more about the Civil Air Patrol by going to:

http://www.gocivilairpatrol.com/cap_home/teens/

The Civil Air Patrol has some annual dues, but they are very reasonable. You will learn a lot in the Civil Air Patrol about aviation. You will not get to fly much, but they will have the senior members take you up once in a Civil Air Patrol aircraft.

When you are 18 you can join the Civil Air Patrol as a Senior Member. There is no maximum age for Senior Members. I was a member of the Civil Air Patrol for several years as a Senior Member.

MICROSOFT FLIGHT SIMULATOR DOES NOT FLY THE SAME AS THE REAL PLANE!

A lot of teens are interested in flying because they have mastered the Microsoft Flight Simulator at home. Although you can learn the basics with MFS, it is not the same as flying the real plane

. I've taken some teens up that had mastered Microsoft and they were real disappointed when they found out they could not really fly the plane. A plane is not a video game and it does not act like a video game!

Microsoft Flight Simulator will help you much more when you get into your instrument training. It does not help you master the flying basics any more than you would be able to master riding a bicycle by playing a game on a computer.

So while Microsoft Flight Simulator can benefit you some by helping you with the flying process and procedure—it will not teach you to fly the plane. You have to get up in a real plane to do that.

REDBIRD SIMULATORS

There is a company down in Texas that makes general aviation simulators that are about as close to the real thing as I have found. The simulator they make is full motion. It is the only full motion simulator for general aviation. The company's name is Redbird.

If you get a chance to spend some time in in Redbird full motion simulator; I believe you will find it worthwhile. You can put the time in your log book, but it does not count towards the required FAA minimum hours. Your flight instructor will have the most up the date information on this.

HAVE A BACK UP PLAN

Aviation has had its ups and downs. When the economy is bad, pilots are laid off. When pilots are laid off, they don't get paid. All pilots have been affected by furloughs or layoffs. All pilots have been unemployed at one time or another. Sometimes this goes on for many years.

The starting pay is very low and has been very low for decades. I do hope and expect that will change in the future. **First year airline pilots qualify for food stamps because they are not paid enough.**

You will also make poverty wages for several years if you flight instruct. The flight schools generally only pay you when you are flying in the airplane. If you are sitting around the flight school all day and have no students then you will not get paid.

Beginning commercial pilots do not make much. I remember flying a trip one day. From the time I left home until I returned home it was about 12 hours. I actually paid the baby sitter more that day, for watching my child, than I had been paid for flying the aircraft as a first officer.

Unfortunately this is reality and you really are going to need a backup plan. Just about every commercial pilot that I know has a side job or side business. That will help some, but it would be better if you planned things out and have the proper expectations.

GET A COLLEGE DEGREE

The best advise that I can give to you is to get a college degree in something that is not aviation related. Get a degree that will provide a living for you and your family. That way you will always have something to fall back on if the aviation gig does not work out.

Actually getting a college degree can fall into a really nice schedule for aviation training. Let me explain my thinking here.

You can not be hired by the airlines until your are 23. In order to be hired by the airlines you need 1500 hours and all of your ratings.

If you start working on your flight training while you are in high school, then by the time you go to college you could have all of your ratings except for the ATP. You can not get the ATP until you are 23.

That will allow you to concentrate on your college studies. You could work part time as a flight instructor while you are in college. This will help build your hours towards the 1500 you will need to get your ATP and get hired by the airlines. You would also make a few bucks doing it instead of spending money furthering your aviation training and career while you are in college.

There is a lot of waiting around time and that will allow you to work on your college studies between students.

UNIVERSITIES

There are about a dozen well known Universities (Embry Riddle, Purdue, University of North Dakota, etc) with 4 year aviation programs.

At the end of the four years you come out with a college degree and your pilot ratings as part of those studies. Many pilots go to one of those universities. The ones that I have spoken with seem to be pleased with their training at these universities.

If you like structure then this might be something that you would be interested in. Universities with aviation programs tend to be very expensive education programs. However you need to remember that you are paying for two items within these programs. You are paying for the college classes just like you would at any college or university and you are also paying for the flight training along with those classes.

Universities are another option for you. The pilot's license you receive after you graduate from one of these universities does not look any different than any other pilot's license.

WHEN & HOW TO DO GROUND SCHOOL

Ground School is also known as classroom time. Although some will disagree, the practical purpose of ground school is to prepare you for the written FAA test, for the rating, you are working on.

You can attend ground school a number of ways.

1. You can get individual instruction from a flight instructor.
2. You can sit in a classroom setting with a number of students and attend ground school while an instructor teaches the class.
3. You can self study using a set of videos
4. You can self study using computer based instruction.

There is no one way that you must do ground school. Some schools teach it. Some don't. Some flight instructors will just tell you to get a set of videos and use those videos to study. There is no specific time you must begin your ground school training. With that being said, I will give you my recommendation on this.

I do not think you should start your ground school training until after you solo. It makes a whole lot more sense to you when you can combine the practical flying with the ground school.

I have seen students take an entire ground school course before they ever get into a plane. In my opinion, this is a complete waste of time. By the time you get into the plane, you have forgotten most of what you were taught and you are going to have to learn it again.

As far as the best way to learn ground school, I'm going to leave that up to you. I have done the classroom, the videos and the computer training method. In my case, the computer training method worked best for me. I had the worst results with the videos.

The most expensive way to do ground school is one on one with an instructor. That might cost you $50+ per hour of ground instruction at some schools. You will need about 40-60 hours. In my opinion you can spend the money better elsewhere.

The least expensive way it with the computer based instruction. That will cost you less than $40 a rating. Just load the software on your laptop or iPad and study for about two weeks every chance you get.

The company that I have used with success, for computer based ground school is Dauntless Aviation. They are on the internet at the following website:

http://www.dauntless-soft.com/

They are very inexpensive and the training worked well for me. I would try Dauntless first because this will be your least expensive way to learn ground school. If it doesn't work, then the most you are out is about the cost of about one hour of flight instruction. If it does work it will save you hundreds or thousands of dollars.

Chapter Eleven

He Who Holds The Gold Rules

There is a saying in business that reads "He Who Holds The Gold Rules."

What it means is that the person that has the money is in charge. If you think about this, it is a very simple concept.

If you turn your money over to your flight school then you are no longer in charge and you can no longer make the rules. The flight school is now in charge of your money and they will make the rules.

Since we do not yet have much flight school regulation in this country you should never let the flight school be in charge of your money. Today flight school tuition is only protected in the states of California, Utah and Tennessee. Even when the tuition is protected, it may still be a while until you get it back if something does go wrong. In addition, you may not get it all back.

You can insure that you continue to make the rules by simply holding onto your money and not letting any flight school hold more than $2500 of your money for deposits and advance payments.

No matter what path you choose to become a professional pilot, I do hope you are successful. Aviation is an incredible profession and offers so many opportunities that are not available elsewhere.

This is an exciting time in the aviation industry. We have just come though a decade of technological advances that are nothing short of amazing. You are going to benefit greatly. You are in the right place at the right time.

You have taken the important first step. You are embarking on a lifelong educational journey.

Welcome Aboard!

www.ingramcontent.com/pod-product-compliance
Lightning Source LLC
Chambersburg PA
CBHW050648160426
43194CB00010B/1856